POVERTY
OR
PLENTY?

POVERTY
OR
PLENTY?

BY

M. N. ROY

GYAN

Published by

Gyan Publishing House
5, Ansari Road
Daryaganj, New Delhi-110002
Phone: 011-47034999, 9811692060
E-mail: books@gyanbooks.com

Distribution Network
gyanbooks.com
India, USA, Canada, UK, Australia

ISBN: 978-93-6280-100-5 (PB)
First Published, 1943

2nd Impression 2024

Printed at: Gyan Press, Delhi.

POVERTY OR PLENTY?
Author: M. N. ROY

POVERTY
OR
PLENTY?

by

M. N. ROY

CONTENTS

I

THE PROBLEM OF PRICE CONTROL

The primary responsibility of a Government is to guard the welfare of the community. Laws are given and rights are established to facilitate the discharge of that fundamental responsibility. If some of those laws and rights are utilised for a purpose harmful to the welfare of the community, the Government is entitled to take any measures for penalising the anti-social act.

The problem of price control ceases to be baffling if the Government takes the view that no right is sacrosanct if it is exercised for an unsocial purpose. The problem is to be approached not from a theoretical point of view, but from the practical point of view of general welfare and public security. The object of controlling prices is not to interfere with any " normal economic law ". It is to control profiteering middlemen making money at the cost of the consumers by interfering with the free exchange of commodities. They are not only victimising the consumers, but are throwing the community in a state of discontent and excitement which is being utilised for dangerous purposes.

Profiteering is an abuse of the legal right of private property. Deprive a selfish minority of the protection of the law which permits such an abuse, and the artificial scarcity will disappear. It should not be very difficult to devise a machinery to guarantee free movement of commodities. Then it may no longer be necessary even to control prices. Operation of the law of supply and demand may be expected to bring down prices to the pre-war level, adjusted to any rise of wages or war-time inflation or any other emergency.

Once the necessity of controlling prices is realised, and the legitimacy of the practice admitted, the problem ceases to be baffling. But all sorts of difficulties could be imagined by those who would start from the assumption that the process of price control is one of the most difficult and complicated methods of interfering with the normal rhythm of the economic life of the community. It is as mystic to assume a normal rhythm of economic life as it is to believe that there is such a thing as eternal and immutable human nature.

No problems of social life can ever be solved if all the rules of conduct are to be approved by *a priori* theories, as all the theories of classical economics are. They may have some bearing upon an imaginary normal state of affairs. But it is absolutely no use appealing to them when we are to deal with abnormal conditions.

For the welfare of the community, it becomes necessary to control prices whenever the movement of prices refuses to follow the normal course which is believed by theoretical economists to be determined by the law of supply and demand. To enumerate theoretical difficulties for remedying the situation, is not exactly a scientific approach to the problem. We must look for the cause of the phenomenon, and simplification is a feature of the scientific method.

Unless there are artificial obstacles in the process of the exchange of commodities, prices rise only when supply cannot cope with demand. Is there such a disparity between supply and demand at present in the country? That is the question which must be replied, to begin with. If there is any disparity, then we must ascertain whether it is caused by greater demand or less supply. That can be easily ascertained, and as soon as that is done, the cause of the phenomenon of uncontrollably rising prices will be laid bare as something abnormal, unreasonable or irrational.

It is obvious that the demand for food stuff, on the whole, has not grown appreciably since the war began. The demand having not increased appreciably, the rise in prices must therefore be caused by inadequate supply. Indeed, that *apparently* is the cause. There is a scarcity. But how is the scarcity caused? Either less food grains are being produced, or part of the total produce is not coming to the market. Nothing has happened since the war began to reduce the production of food grains. Except for about a million men joining the army, there has been no withdrawal of labour from agriculture. The displacement of labour caused by the expansion of industries is also negligible. On the other hand, war conditions have discouraged the growing of commercial crops for export. Consequently, food must be grown now on some more land. Finally, there has been no large-scale crop failure.[1]

This brief analysis of the situation leads only to one conclusion. The present scarcity and the resulting rise of prices are caused not by any appreciable fall of production, *but by some artificial* obstacles to the free movement of

[1] Estimated area under important food crops and their estimated yield. (*Indian Trade Journal,* Summary of Food Forecasts).

		1939-40	1940-41	1941-42	1942-43
Rice	(000 acres)	74,255	73,059	73,575	75,193
,,	(000 tons)	25,800	22,150	25,351	24,696
Wheat	(000 acres)	34,003	34,862	33,979	34,311
,,	(000 tons)	10,784	10,005	10,070	—

An increase of 23 per cent in rice crop is estimated for 1943-44, compared to 1942-43.

commodities. The normal operation of the law of supply and demand is being interfered with. As a matter of fact, this law never operates normally. So long as exchange of commodities is guided primarily by profit motive, and this is respected as sacrosanct, demand can never be supplied freely. Supply is held up to create a more pressing (as against a greater) demand, which forces up prices.[2] That is trade.

The Government, however, assumes that there is a greater demand. Addressing the Sixth Price Control Conference on September 7, 1942, the Commerce Member of the Government of India said: "The main task before us is to adjust our total supplies of food stuff and other essential commodities to the ever increasing demands, and to ensure their equitable distribution." Then he proceeded to enumerate "the chief factors which are responsible for the increased demand over and above normal consumption." They are: (1) large-scale purchases on behalf of the army; (2) supply for neighbouring countries like Ceylon; (3) increase in money incomes as the result of the manyfold activities in connection with the war; (4) strategic reserves built by the provincial and State Governments; and (5) hoarding of large stocks in the absence of control over the entire available supplies of food stuff and their distribution by the State.

A little analysis will show that none of the first four factors, or even all of them taken together, could essentially increase the volume of real demand. The apparent dis-

[2] Cases of an artificial restriction of supply are not lacking in the present day restrictive economy. Destruction of supply, deliberate control and restriction of the same, the various international commodity conferences and the quota system, and the whole concept of technological unemployment with its emphasis on controlled scientific advancement have all been the symptoms of this malady.

parity between supply and demand is really caused by the fifth factor, which the Commerce Member dismissed with the following remark: "Although such stocks create difficulties in the immediate present and raise prices, they are like hidden reserves which will be ultimatelly available for the community."[3] This amounts to exonerating the real culprit. When the hidden reserves held by them will be ultimately available, according to their convenience, it may be already too late.

Before proceeding to show, on the basis of the report of the successive price control conferences convened by the Government of India, that these "hidden reserves" are the real cause of the artificial scarcity and the resulting higher prices, let us examine the other factors enumerated by the Commerce Member, which are generally believed to be the cause of the present short supply of food stuffs and other essential commodities.

The purchases on behalf of the army represent operation of a part of the old demand through a different channel. The men who have now joined the army had to be fed previously. Therefore, now the Government is simply purchasing a quantity of food which used to be bought by individual consumers who have now joined the armed forces. The demand is increased by this factor only to the extent that food enough for feeding the army perhaps for a couple of years is being held in reserve. That certainly is not a very large increase of demand in relation to the total production of food. But this slight increase in demand is

---

[3] It is now accepted on all hands that the rise in prices in the first few months after the war began was speculative in character. "These price increases were primarily due to the growth of speculative inventories in the expectation of a further rise in prices". (*War and Indian Economic Policy*, page 13).

counter-balanced by the stoppage of practically all commercial export. Increasing demand caused by the necessity of supplying neighbouring countries is also upset by the stoppage of commercial export.[4]

The strategic reserve built up by Provincial and State Governments do indeed withhold some commodities from

[4] "Since statements are still appearing in the press that heavy exports of food grains from India, and from Bengal in particular, are continuing, the Government of India wish to state categorically that there is no foundation for such statements. The total exports of food grains from India during 1942-43 was 370,000 tons, representing a steady decrease from the 1937-38 figure of over 900,000 tons. Since the beginning of 1943 the monthly export figures (in tons) from India have been as follows:

January	140	13,830	13,970
February	166	19,058	19,224
March	6	12,612	12.618
April	33	7,819	7,852
May	216	5,479	5,695
June	20,321	10,166	30,487
July	283	2,008	2,291
Total	21,165	70,972	92,137

Over the same period the total exports of rice by sea and by rail from Bengal have been less than 7,000 tons of which exports outside India were less than 3,000 tons in January. Against this there were imports into Bengal of 70,000 tons, representing net imports of 63,000 tons. These figures are specially significant in view of the extremely acute food crisis prevalent in Bengal practically throughout the year 1943.

"It has often been publicly alleged that the requirements of the defence services are a very severe drain on India's resources of foodgrains. The Government of India wish to state that the total annual requirements of the Defence Services in India of wheat and rice are 500,000 tons and 144,000 tons respectively. To see these figures in the proper perspective it should be observed that they represent only one-eighth of the total amount of wheat produced in a year in the Punjab alone, and only one-sixtieth of the total annual average production of rice in Bengal. If it is necessary for any operational reasons to transport any quantity of those Defence Services foodgrains overseas, that quantity comes out of the quotas mentioned above and is not additional to them." (*Times of India*, August, 23, 1943.)

the market. But it would be foolish for those Governments to build up those reserves at the cost of the consumer, because that would be to risk the present for guaranteeing the future. Therefore, it can be assumed that those reserves are kept within the limits of prudence and reason, and cannot be the cause of artificial scarcity.

The other factor of increase in money incomes is purely theoretical. It can operate only in the case of a very small fraction of the people. Therefore, even if it were operative to any appreciable extent, the increase in demand would be almost negligible. Only wage-earners come into account here. Whatever increase in money income may have accrued to them during the war, that does not represent any rise in real wages, which have fallen heavily owing to the higher cost of living. The practically negligible increase in their money income has not done anything more than partially compensate for their declining real income. The total amount of money paid in wages to-day may be larger than that paid before the war. But it buys much less than it used to do previously. Therefore, on the whole, the factor of increased incomes has not been in operation at all.

Now let us revert to the factor which is the real cause of scarcity. The Commerce Member made the following remark in this connection: "In the absence of control over the entire available supplies of food stuffs, and their distribution by the State, consumers and producers tend to hoard large stocks either as a result of their psychological reaction to the uncertainties of the war conditions, or in the hope of getting higher prices in future." Again, the real culprit is exonerated. The trader is the most dominating factor in the economic life of this country in so far as food stuff is concerned. He acquires that dominating position, on the one hand, owing to the economic bankruptcy of the producers who are mostly small peasants, and, on the other hand, because of the poverty of the vast bulk of consumers. The majority of the producers are simply not in a position to hoard agricultural commodities in their possession for any length of time. They require money to pay rent, meet the creditor's demands, and to buy manufactured goods. Therefore, they are compelled to part with their products as soon as the harvest is collected. Hoarding on any large scale is therefore possible only in the case of a small number of producers. Consequently, hoarding by producers owing to one reason or another cannot seriously reduce the supply. As regards the consumers, the vast majority of them in this country are known to live from hand to mouth. Few of them possess the wherewithal to lay in any large stock. That being the case, hoarding, which is certainly the cause of the present scarcity, is done by the traders, and then again, by the whole-sale dealers who can afford to have large sums of money locked up over a period of time. That is exactly what is happening. And that is the problem to be solved.

The nature of the problem will become clear in the light of the report of the successive Price Control Conferences convened by the Government since the beginning of the war. Immediately after the outbreak of the war, there was an abrupt rise in retail prices. Evidently, the factors enumerated by the Commerce Member were not in operation at that time. Nevertheless, the rise was so sharp as to require the Government to fix prices of certain necessities of life such as food stuffs, salt, kerosene oil, and the cheaper qualities of cotton cloth. The first Price Conrol Conference was held in the middle of October 1939. The general opinion of the conference was that it was not necessary to check the rise in the prices of agricultural products. Indeed, agricultural prices need not be held on the level of that time, if the benefit of the rise was going to the cultivator. The weekly index price at that time was 111·4 compared to the pre-war price. But presently, it became evident that the benefit was not reaching the cultivator. As a matter of fact, neither the consumers nor the producers being represented on the conference, the opinion of the latter could be determined only by the interests of the traders who alone were represented there, in addition to the representatives of the Central Provincial and State Governments.

In December 1939, that is, a month and a half after the First Price Control Conference, the weekly index number of prices rose to 139·9. Evidently, profiteering was encouraged by the attitude of *laissez faire* taken up by the First Price Control Conference. But the Government could not disregard the continuation of the sharp rise of prices, and the Second Price Control Conference was convened at the end of January 1940. Even then the general opinion of the Conference was against interference with the rise in the prices of agricultural products. But it was not due to any concern to help the producer. Because, it was agreed to fix the prices at which wholesale dealers were to buy from the producers. Of course, the corollary to that agreement could not be avoided, and the prices in the wholesale market had also to be fixed. But a large loophole was left. In order to reach the consumer, the commodities must pass through a whole series of middlemen after they have gone out of the wholesale market. Unless prices were controlled in all those intervening stages, the consumer could never get any benefit of the control. So, a system of control was introduced, which benefitted neither the consumer, on the one hand, nor the producer, on the other. In other words, it was a system which benefitted only the small class of traders. The responsibility of controlling prices in the intermediate stages of exchange was placed on Provincial and State Governments, which were given very large discretion. The result was complete nullification of any effective control of prices in so far as the bulk of the consumers was concerned.

Nevertheless, the very fact of introducing control in order to check the sharp rise in prices had a sobering effect. Throughout the year 1940, the prices generally declined. It should be noted that by that time all the factors enumerated by the Commerce Member had come into operation. Nor had there been any substantial increase in production. Yet, by February 1941, the index number of prices went down to 109·7. Evidently, the sharp rise of prices in the previous year had been due to profiteering, which had gone to the extent of withholding so much stock as could not be subsequently thrown in the market without bringing down prices. Most probably, a considerable part of the hoarding was done by middlemen who could keep their money locked up indefinitely; or perhaps they were afraid that the control system might be tightened if the situation did not improve.

However, presently it became clear that it was a fluctuation caused by speculative practice. Having touched the low figure of 109.7 in February 1941, prices again began to rise, and reached 138·3 in September of the same year. The Government was evidently alarmed. In June 1941, the power to control prices already delegated to the Provincial Governments was strengthened by the delegation of power to prohibit the withholding from sale of articles whose prices were controlled. Presiding over the Third Price Control Conference held in the middle of October 1941, the then Commerce Member of the Government of India, Sir A. Ramaswami Mudaliar, said that there was no real scarcity of food stuff. Nevertheless, he felt called upon to observe that "the question of wheat prices has to be carefully watched," and added that "it might be possible, or even necessary, for the Central Government to intervene at any stage if there is a tendency for a rise in the price of wheat." That was obviously a recognition of the fact that profiteering was the cause of higher prices.

The warning had not been given any too soon, because the wheat problem continued to grow in seriousness. So much so, that in the beginning of November the Government issued a press note warning traders that anybody selling wheat at a price higher than Rs. 4/6 would do so at his own risk. But the warning did not discourage profiteering and speculative practice. Ultimately, the Government issued a definite order on December 5, 1941, fixing the maximum price for wheat at Rs. 4/6. But even then a loophole was left. The Provincial Governments were authorised to determine the maximum price for their respective local markets, "having regard for the normal relation between prices at such places", and the central markets That discretion for the Provincial Governments was bound to deprive the consumers of the benefit of price control. Because, "regard to the normal relation" of prices at the central market and loral markets meant concession to the traders. The latter were to be allowed to have their pound of flesh.

The Fourth Price Control Conference, held in February

1942, took notice of the transport difficulties which interfered with free movement of commercial goods. On the pretext of those difficulties, the control system was decentralised, which enabled local hoarding and the consequent shortage in provinces which depend on food stuff grown in other provinces.

At last the real nature of the problem had to be admitted in the Fifth Price Control Conference, held in April 1942. The conference emphasised the vital importance of linking control of distribution with price control, and recommended the introduction of the licensing of wholesale dealers. It was believed that the system of licensing would enable Provincial and State Governments to get information regarding the course of distribution of food grains, and minimise the evil of hoarding. But the discretion of licensing the retail dealers was again left to the Provincial Governments. The nature of the problem was grasped, but the approach was defective. Consequently, it proved still to be baffling. There was no reason for adopting that half-measure. Because, the Government appeared to be fully alive to the danger of the situation. Soon after the Fifth Price Control Conference, the Government issued orders for checking speculative dealings which were believed to be partly responsible for the rise of prices, even against the prescribed maximum.

The experience of two years' ineffective efforts shows that the problem is not of production, but of distribution. The scarcity is artificially created. The "Grow More Food" campaign is a mechanical imitation of the practice in Britain which is largely dependent upon imported food. In this country, the campaign only serves the purpose of hiding the real culprit. In the midst of an artificially created scarcity, any effective control of prices is not possible strictly within the frame work of the system of "normal" trade. Yet, all price control measures introduced hitherto have been so framed as to allow the "freedom of trade". But subject to the freedom of trade, no practical effort to control prices is ever possible. Because, effective price control necessarily amounts to interference with "normal" trade, and consequently means encroachment upon the sacred right of private property. Unless the Government can get over that prejudice, all efforts to control prices will be abortive.

The grain in the godown of the dealer is his property. Since it belongs to him, he may or may not sell it ; or sell it wherever and whenever he likes. Once this proprietary right of private individuals is admitted, there is no room for any control of the movement of prices. Because, the prices will necessarily rise or fall according to the whims of the trader ; or, more correctly speaking, the movement of prices will be determined by the profit motive. Prices of commodities cannot be controlled without controlling the motive of their legal owner to make profit at the cost of the consumer.

Freedom of trade enables the trader to create *legally* artificial scarcity by withholding food and other necessities from the market, and later on sell them at a higher price. That practice is called profiteering. That is exactly what is happening. And that is the problem to be solved.

Addressing the Sixth Price Control Conference on September 7 1942, the Commerce Member stated the problem as such. He said: "The distribution of food stuffs is as vital a part of the food policy as production. Mere fixation of maximum prices cannot ensure that the consumer will in practice get the commodities at the controlled rate. So long as the private trader controls supplies, there is always an incentive for him to charge higher price than the legal maximum." But at the same time, he reassured the private trader that "the proposed price control scheme does not seek to eliminate the existing trade channels, but they are made an integral part of the scheme." That is the surest way of defeating your own object.

Apparently, the opposition to stricter price control is mainly due to a concern for the well-being of the peasantry. The general opinion in the first two Price Control Conferences was against any interference with the rise in the basic prices of agricultural products. Only in the third conference, it was felt that it might be necessary to intervene if there was a tendency for a rise in the price of wheat. And soon afterwards, the wholesale price for wheat was fixed. But since then, the food situation went on deteriorating, and ultimately the sixth conference could no longer avoid the unpleasant task of visualising effective control. On that occasion, the Commerce Member declared: "The necessity is being increasingly felt for more drastic measures against profiteering in every form."

Incidentally, he revealed the real nature of the problem. It was profiteering, which has to be checked. Control of prices alone, however drastic, cannot deal with this problem. Because of that reason, the system of price control has not produced the desired results. Therefore, all opposition to the system is due not to any concern for the producer, but for the middleman.

However, it may be useful to see how far the peasantry in benefitted by the higher prices of agricultural products. In his speech at the Sixth Price Control Conference, the

Commerce Member mentioned two objections to control. They are: (1) It is unfair to control the prices of what the agriculturist produces, while the prices of products he consumes remain uncontrolled ; (2) Adequate attention is not paid to the increase in the cultivator's cost of living and production. Apparently, the objections are very plausible. If the benefit of higher prices really went to the peasants, then they should not be regarded as an unmixed evil. Indeed, taking a longer view of things, they should be welcome. Because more money in the pocket of the peasant would increase his purchasing power, thus laying down a sound foundation for national economy. That asset would be valuable enough to make some immediate hardships worthwhile. If the peasantry is left out of account, the consuming public, which suffers from higher prices is numerically very small. It is composed of the urban middle-class and industrial wage-earners. In India, the two together do not constitute more than ten per cent of the population. In relation to them, the problem of higher prices would become less baffling. The solution would then be found in correspondingly higher wages and dearness allowance.

As a matter of fact, the peasantry is not benefitted by the higher prices of agricultural products. Whatever little benefit accrues to them, is more than counter-balanced by the higher prices of other necessities. Therefore, the problem of higher prices affects practically the entire population, and as such it is bound to be baffling, because it is artificially created.

On the face of it, the rise in the prices of agricultural products has only kept pace with the rise in the prices of manufactured commodities. In the latter case, the rise has been of approximately a hundred per cent. The average price of wheat, for example, during the five years preceding the war was Rs. 2/8. Now the wholesale price has been fixed at Rs. 5/-. That is also a hundred per cent rise. But very little of this increase reaches the actual cultivator. Before the wheat comes to the wholesale market, it passes through more than one middleman. It is well known that there is a big disparity between the wholesale price and the price at which wheat and other agricultural products are bought from the cultivator. In any case, the peasant gets only a small share of the higher price. On the other hand, he has to bear the full burden of the rise in the price of manufactured articles. If the control is removed, the price of agricultural products will rise higher. But there is no ground for the assumption that the peasantry would be benefitted thereby any more than under the system of the present controlled price. The result will be greater hardship for the rest of the population.

The professed concern for the welfare of the peasantry thus can be dismissed as a ground for the objection to stricter control of agricultural prices. Under no circumstances, prices have any direct relation with production. They are determined by competition, which takes place in the realm of exchange of commodities. Therefore, any control of price means some restriction on what is considered to be the freedom of trade. That being the case, concern for the traders' interest is the real ground for the objection to price control. That is very clear from the analysis of the situation given in the Commerce Member's speech to the Sixth Price Control Conference. He said: "So long as the controlling authority does not control the supply of commodities and their distribution, and is not in a position to sell in the market large quantities through recognised trade agencies at the controlled rates, the legal maximum cannot be made effective over a large range of the market. Control over supply and distribution are therefore essential and vital corollaries to effective price control." The flaw in this very correct annalysis of the problem is to allot to "recognised trade agencies" any place in the system of control. Prices forced up artificially by profiteering can be controlled only through competition. That is to say, by selling at a lower price. When traders are conspiring against public interest, the Government should "sell in the market large quantities" of necessities *directly*. As soon as "trade agencies" are given any place, the "legitimate" share of the trader must be admitted. That is to say, the element of profit would creep in, and the rate of profit is always determined by the trader, who can invent all sorts of convenient excuses. If by the term "recognised trade agencies" the Commerce Member meant Co-operative Societies, for example, then he certainly hit upon the right solution of the problem.

The opening of other channels of distribution than trade suggests itself as the only solution of the problem, particularly when it is restated as done by the Commerce Member himself. He said that it was a problem of "black" markets, and declared that "the proposed modifications in our scheme of price control would eliminate the black market." He went on to mention that "in England even the help of the Scotland Yard has had to be requisitioned for combating this menace, and the black market in that country has come to be branded as the traitor's market". If a similar view of the situation is taken by the authorities in this country, it should not be difficult to find a correct approach to the problem, and there should be no hesitation in taking the drastic measures warranted for the protection of public welfare.

The following propositions result logically from an impartial analysis of the food situation: Without trade control, there can be no price control; any successful control of prices presupposes restriction on the freedom of trade. In the last analysis, it is a choice between public welfare and private interest.

But there seem to be differences in high quarters about the view of situation which was taken by the Sixth Price Control Conference. It is rumoured that the matter came up for discussion in the Viceroy's Executive Council, and some Members advocated stricter control. Others, led by Sir Jogendra Singh, are reported to have objected, indeed pressed for the abolition of all control, presumably on the familiar ground that the peasantry should not be deprived of the benefit of higher agricultural prices. Not is there any secret about it. Sir Jogendra Singh expressed his views in the last meeting of the Council of State. But is he really ignorant of the fact that the big landlords of Punjab are holding large stocks of wheat, evidently with the purpose of coering the Government to raise the prices? According to a recent report, those landlords have created a syndicate, presumably in anticipation of a new scheme of control said to be under the consideration of the Central Government. The new scheme proposes to authorise only six dealers to purchase wheat, and then supply it to the Controllers of Supply in the provinces for distribution again through authorized dealers. There seems to be a rivalry between the landlords and merchants for the spoils of profiteering. Inside the Government, this rivalry is likely to operate through the Land Department, on the one hand, and the Departments of Commerce and Supply, on the other. However, the new system, if introduced, cannot be expected to improve the situation. The entire system of control would be subordinated to trading interest. Therefore, the Punjab landlords are embattling themselves. They are constituting themselves into a commercial syndicate, confident of being recognised as one of the six authorized dealers.

The merit of the new scheme will be, it is maintained, to eliminate competition among dealers purchasing from the producers. Elimination of competition at that stage will operate against the peasants. So, all the professed concern for the poor peasants is nothing more that the proverbial crocodile's tears. On the other hand, those who are of the opinion that the entire price structure will be steadier if the price of agricultural products could be fixed at the stage of purchase from the producer, are still laying the blame at the door of the peasants, who have absolutely no voice anywhere.

If the peasants would be compelled to sell only to a restricted number of authorised purchasers, the latter would be in a position to dictate the price. Consequently, the peasantry would be even worse off than to-day. On the other hand, the authorised dealers would be priviledged to have a practical monopoly over the whole field of supply. The Government Controllers of Supply would be in a helpless position, sandwiched between a few monopolist authorised dealers, on the one hand, and by an army of authorised retail dealers, on the other. One need not have much imagination to see how the food situation will be extremely aggravated if this new system is introduced.

An over-estimation of the place of the trader in the system of distribution is preventing the authorities from approaching the problem in the most obvious way. Since higher prices are mainly due to profiteering, it is evident that the problem cannot be solved with the help of those who are exactly creating it. It is not an ethical question. There are not good traders and bad traders. Traders are traders, and they may be all good or all bad. Trade has a function, and that is to make profit. And profit can be made by creating artificial scarcity.

In his address to the Sixth Price Control Conference, the Commerce Member actually visualised the problem in that setting. Yet, he could not think of tackling the problem without the goodwill and co-operation of the traders. He addressed a passionate appeal to them: "I shall soon meet representatives of the commercial community and have the opportunity of making an earnest appeal to them to assist Government in the matter and discharge the responsibility which they owe to society and the country by virtue of the position of influence held by them in our present economic and social structure." It is true that the commercial community happens to have a great influence over the present economic life of the country. But it is also true that they are not exercising this influence to promote social welfare. If they did that, there would be no food problem and the necessity of price control would not arise. For, it has been shown earlier in this article that there is no such disparity between supply and demand as normally causes rise in prices.

The distribution of necessities is a social function. For ages, this function has been performed by the trader. But from that it does not necessarily follow that trade is the only channel of distribution. One of the beneficial results of this war may be to compel the opening up of other, less wasteful, more equitable channels of distribution. So long as the trader performs a social function by conveying commodities from the producer to the consumer, there should be no objection to his being recompensed for the services rendered. Only in that sense the trader's profit is justifiable. But then it is nothing more than wages, and as wages it should be proportionate to the labour performed. But the trader's profit is not calculated on the basis of the social utility of his service. The freedom of trade gives him the freedom of charging as much as the traffic can bear. The recognition of the inviolability of the right of private property precludes any restriction in his freedom. Consequently, originally a useful social function, trade in course of time came to be an instrument for explotation. It exploits by its delinquency in doing what is its social duty. Instead of conveying the commodities from the producer to the consumer, it withholds them from the latter. That delinquency in respect of a social duty is the foundation of the traders' profit as it is known to-day. The dividing line between that delinquency, committed even during normal times, and profiteering during emergencies, is very difficult to fix. Consequently, profiteering can also be justified as nothing more than traders making profit. That being the case, the present food situation cannot be remedied with the goodwill and co-operation of the traders.

If it was possible to persuade or compel the trader to revert to his original position, he could be fitted into a sheme of control necessary for protecting the public. But evidently that is not possible. That is the lesson of the experience of three years, and the same experience has been made in all other countries during this war. If the State could adopt drastic measures, as in England, for example, then the necessity of opening up of an alternative channel for distribution might not be so urgent. But because of the influential position of the trader in the economic life of this country, the State seems to be helpless. Therefore, the solution of the problem is to be sought in other directions.

And that is not altogether an innovation. Consumers' Co-operatives have proved to be very efficient and beneficial channels of distribution. They are bound to replace private trade. By fostering their growth, the Government could cope with the situation with the goodwill and co-operation of an immensely larger section of the community than the small privilaged class of traders. This approach to the problem should commend itself to the authorities, because it does not involve any departure from conventional notions nor go against any pet prejudice. The idea of taking drastic measures against profiteering is repugnant to those for whom private property is sacrosanct. But the evil of profiteering cannot be cured by tinkering. At the same time, the food situation can be allowed to drift only at the risk of the Government themselves. Therefore, they would be wise to adopt the constructive policy of fomenting the growth of Co-operative Societies and give them greater importance in the field of distribution, if they are still unable to gather the courage for commiting the revolutionary act of dealing firmly with a small privileged class which is deliberately undermining the home front, when the shadow of invasion is cast athwart the country.

The question of food supply should not be treated out of the context of the entire political and military situation. In Britain, it has been placed in the forefront of the war efforts. It should be treated similarly in this country, and and the solution here should be simpler. Because, in the last analysis, there is no food scarcity in this country. Therefore, the idea of creating a Food Supply Department in the Government of India should be welcomed. But it should be an independent Department, headed by a popular man capable of resisting the influence of the powerful privileged classes who are creating the problem of food supply. The effort must be made in two directions simultaneously. On the one side, trade must be controlled and the rigor of the control must increase progressively ; on the other side, the alternative channel of distribution should be opened by promoting the organisation of Co-operative Societies throughout the country. In order to be fully effective, agricultural producers should be organised in Co-operatives for selling products. There is a good chance of the economic life of the country being thus reorganised and rationalised under the impact of war emergency. Let not the chance be missed.

Oct. 18, 1942.

II

DEMOCRACY *VERSUS* CAPITALISM

The London Chamber of Commerce Report on post-war reconstruction pleads for "a twentieth century economic system", and recommends rejection of "the mentality of the nineteenth century economists who assumed that the only proper object of an economic system was to produce the maximum of real wealth with the minimum of labour, and therefore looked to division of labour carried to its extreme limit, not only as between people within the nation, but as between one nation and another." That is a bold and frank admission that after the war economic status quo cannot be re-established. The admission not only amounts to a condemnation of Imperialism, but to a realisation of the limitations of capitalism. The world devastated by this war cannot be reconstructed economically, and therefore otherwise, on the basis of economic relations which constituted the foundation of the achievements of modern civilisation during the eighteenth and nineteenth centuries. A special committee set up by the London Chamber of Commerce has come to that conclusion.[1] Lest they are forgotten, some of the thought-provoking passages of the highly significant report may be recapitulated.

> "It is widely admitted that there was something radically wrong with our economic system. It was palpably absurd that nations should be desperate-

[1] The importance of the source from which these views have been expressed can hardly be overemphasised. The London Chamber of Commerce has a direct membership of 9,000 firms and companies. (*The Economist*, June, 6, 1942.)

ly anxious to export more of their real wealth to other nations than they received in return. It was equally absurd that men in want of the necessaries of life should be denied the money with which to buy them, because there was a superabundance of those necessaries, and therefore their services were not required to make more. There has not, however, been the same readiness to recognise that there must be a serious error in our economic thinking in order to produce in action absurd results.

"The London Chamber of Commerce submits that it is now essential, if greater disasters are to be avoided, so to change the system as to ensure that international trade shall tend to raise the standard of living of the backward nations to that of the advanced nations.

"Unless international trade is changed from a struggle by the nations to get one another into unpayable debt, to a mutually advantageous exchange of real wealth, and unless the palpable absurdity of unemployment and poverty in juxtaposition is permenantly removed, then fear, resentment and frustration, which these things have spread through the world, will destroy our civilisation. Economic systems were made for men, not men for economic systems. Political freedom is not enough. Nations now realise that so long as there is financial and economic domination, political freedom is an illusion.

"We are engaged in a war which is a war of ideas. It is not enough to be negative, to expose and fight false ideas, although this is essential. When we can offer humanity a system which provides economic security and freedom, without the surrender of political freedom as a condition, we shall have armed ourselves with so powerful a weapon of propaganda as to ensure speedy victory. We shall have captured the imagina-

> tion and enthusiastic support of men everywhere. General professions of good intentions after the war will not again be accepted. The necessary changes must be made now."

Having regard for the importance of the quarters from which the above pronouncement is made, it can be confidently expected that in post-war Britain democracy will outgrow the limitations of capitalism.[2] The far-reaching implications of the "twentieth century economic system" may not as yet be realised even by those who advocate it. But they have certainly realised the absurdities of the nineteenth century economic thinking, and the realisation is not a matter of theoretical understanding, but of bitter experience. Therefore, a serious attempt will be made to remove those absurdities, at least partially. That will amount to a re-adjustment of economic relations which constituted the basis of orthodox capitalism.

Political freedom has come within the reach of India, thanks to the new economic thinking which is asserting itself in Britain. Capitalism, guided by the antiquated economic thought of the nineteenth century, was the foundation of modern Imperialism. Therefore, rejection of the nineteenth century economic thinking, even if the advance towards "a twentieth century economic system" will be halting, is bound to cause the disappearance of Imperialism. As a matter of fact, the process has already begun, and it is sure to be accelerated by the exigencies of the problems of the post-war reconstruction of Britain.

India is already feeling the impact of that process. Not only is she becoming free of her "unpayable indebtedness",

---

[2] This is obvious from the nature of the changes taking place in Great Britain in the midst of the present war. Refer in this connection to the article on Planned Economy. (Chapter VIII.)

but she is actually becoming a creditor of Britain.[3] But the impact of new economic thoughts, provoked by the re-adjustment of economic relations, is not yet felt in this country.

Until now the war has been a very good business for the Indian capitalists. It is, therefore, only natural for them to be fully satisfied with the present position and dream of a "free India" which they will rule as the heir-designates of passing Imperialism. Prosperity makes them short-sighted. They believe that political power will enable them to maintain the *status quo* in India, which may be a thing of the past in other parts of the world. But the most curious feature of the Indian situation is the anxiety of the Government to put capitalism in the saddle. The men at the helm of affairs do not seem to realise that this anxiety is not only antagonistic to Indian democracy, but also to the new economic thought gaining ground in Britain.

India's debts to Britain having been paid up almost completely, new sterling balances will accumulate in London to the credit of India. Any attempt for a transfer of those sterling balances during the war will cause a serious financial dislocation. Fear of political complications has compelled the Government of India to disown any intention of using up the credit in London, as in the case of the last war, namely, by making a gift to the war chest. So, after the war, India will have a large credit in Britain. The latter will

[3] India's freeing herself from the "unpayable indebtedness" is clear from the change that has taken place in the composition of her national debt. Her sterling debt has decreased by Rs. 26.61 crores in 1939-40, Rs 97.56 crores in 1940-41, Rs. 164.93 crores in 1941-42, and the estimated decrease in 1942-43 is Rs. 117.33 crores. Thus the entire sterling debt would be cleared off by the end of the present year. Even after this repayment has taken place, it is expected from the huge accumulations of sterling with the Reserve Bank, that we shall have a large credit against Britain (estimated at Rs. 950 crores by March, 1944.)

be able to pay only in one way—by exporting goods. But that time may well be the actual as well as virtual rulers of this country. Protectionism has always been the central plank of the economic platform of nationalism. A national-capitalist State will surely raise high tariff walls for protecting home industries. British goods particularly will be excluded. That will certainly have a serious repercussion on the economic life of Britain and the problems of post-war reconstruction will be correspondingly more complicated.

These considerations should carry weight with the British Government, and their approach to the Indian problem should be accordingly determined. But the present Government of India still refuses to have truck with anybody but the capitalists and their political spokesmen, who consequently behave as its heir-designates.

The strong attitude of the Government towards the Congress does not represent a departure from the policy of placing Indian capitalism in the saddle. As a matter of fact, the debacle of the Congress has clarified the position. The heir-designates no longer operate through "popular" politicians. They have taken things in their own hand. Recently, big business has occupied the centre of the Indian political scene. Of course, businessmen have no time for practising politics. For them, time is money. They want others to practise politics for them. Therefore, big business has openly taken the political arena not to become politicians themselves, but to help their political spokesmen extricate themselves from the difficult situation created by themselves. They are demanding the release of their Mahatma and assuring the Government that, if he is released, he will persuade his blundering followers to mend their ways. That is clearly the meaning of the statement issued by the "Leaders' Conference" in Bombay. As long as the Government remains wedded to the nineteenth century economic ideas, it will not be able to resist the temptation offered by the statement. The Government may have made up its mind no longer to have any truck with the Congress leaders. But it is doubtful whether it will be able to resist the pressure of the industrial and commercial magnates who have agreed to guarantee good behaviour on the part of their political spokesmen, if the latter will be given yet another chance.

Why does the Government of India persist in the policy of placating Indian capitalism, even when it is admitted in powerful quarters in Britain that such a policy is antagonistic to democracy and will prejudice all plans of post-war economic reconstruction? Because the men at the helm of affairs have for years been out of touch with the thought-currents in Britain. Most of them came to this country with nineteenth century ideas. In their official capacity or commercial pursuits, they were associated with Indians under the influence of even more antiquated ideas. It is not possible to tackle new problems with an old mentality. Consequently, the problems of the present Indian situation baffle the men at the helm of affairs who simply cannot conceive of a really democratic regime ever being established in this country, even if they are so very scrupulous about constitutional formalities.

In their hidebound respectability, fortified by old-fashioned notions, they may not be willing to attach any importance to the advice of people who do not belong to their charmed circle. But the London Chamber of Commerce is not exactly a conclave of communist conspirators. The carefully considered and cautiously expressed opinion of that body, which until now provided the sanction for the

British Government of this country, can be disregarded by the latter only at the cost not only of the welfare of the Indian people, but also of the welfare of Britain. A few words about the role of capitalism may help the people at the helm of affairs to discharge their responsibility creditably.[4]

The merit of any economic system is to be judged by its social usefulness. Human society is not a static thing. Ever since the dawn of history, it has been evolving from one stage to another. In each stage, its requirements were different from the previous stage. The object of any economic system is to meet those requirements. Therefore, in each stage of evolution, human society had a specific economic system. Capitalism happened to be the economic system which could satisfy the requirements of human society in one particular stage of evolution. To maintain that, capitalism cannot be replaced, or should not be replaced, by another economic system, is to say that human development came to an end when capitalism became the prevailing economic system. No sensible man would maintain that. Therefore, capitalism must be regarded as a passing show. So long as it satisfied the requirements of society, it was difficult, except for the few who could see

[4] "Pure, undiluted capitalism, no longer possible in the modern world, is still less practicable in India, where private capitalism has so far failed to develop the key, basic and defence industries which must be established quickly. Considering their national importance and the dangers of creating vested interests, it is necessary that such basic industries should be controlled by the state. It may not be necessary for the state to own all industries, but it may be enough for the state to control the key industries (eg. metals, machine tools, machinery, heavy engineering and heavy chemicals) and to allow private capital to be invested therein. On the other hand, Government should nationalise all public utility industries, at least in regard to the future and exexcise control over them.' (P. S. Lokanathan—*Industrialisation*, page 28.)

ahead of time, to visualise that eventually it would exhaust all its possibilities, to be replaced by another economic system better suited for meeting the greater requirements of society on a higher level. But ultimately, the limitations of capitalism became a matter of experience, and the necessity for a new economic system was felt. The limitations and contradictions of capitalism were evident already from the beginning of this century. As a matter of fact, they brought about the last great war. But once a faith is established, it defies experience. Therefore, the world had to live though the troubles and tribulations of the period during the two wars, and experience the great shock of this war, before it could outgrow the venerable prejudices of the nineteenth century.

Political democracy was established during the period when capitalism flourished. Consequently, the two became associated in the mind of the average man. Without capitalism, there can be no democracy: that is the venerable notion of the nineteenth century. But the bubble has been burst by the experience of the twentieth century. It is no longer necessary to swear by Karl Marx. The London Chamber of Commerce has pronounced the death sentence of capitalism. And it has done so with the powerful argument that without economic freedom, political freedom is a myth. In other words, democracy is not possible under capitalism. Because, instead of freeing man economically, capitalism only creates absurdities so graphically described in the Report of the London Chamber of Commerce. And those absurdities only mean economic bondage, social insecurity, privations, hardships, degradation and brutalisation for the masses of man kind.

Can capitalism do anything better for India? The

answer need not be theoretical. While Indian capitalists have been prospering owing to the war, the Indian people are making their experience of the absurdities of capitalism. Perhaps the greatest absurdity of our time is the "scarcity" of food in India. It is an absurdity, because it is artificially created, and it is a creation of capitalism.

Imperialism may be in the process of disappearance. But for the moment, the Government of the country has unlimited power. It could solve the problem of the distribution of food and other primary necessities by one stroke of pen, if it had the courage to do so.[5] But it won't enforce the Defence of India Rules against the capitalists. If hunger and privation drive the people to revolt, the forces

[5] The following editorial comment from the *Times of India*, dated August, 20, 1943, is *typical* of what the press has on occasions written about the food crisis in the country. "The public on seeing 'corpses in the street are requested to inform the nearest police station. Special arrangements have been made for the speedy issue of disposal orders three times a day at the three morgues.' This recent police statement in Calcutta might seem unnecessarily ghoulish were it not for the fact that on the first four days of this week 256 people found suffering from starvation or sickness' on the city's streets were taken to hospital. 21 of them died. Nor does this complete the tale ; as a correspondent in a Calcutta contemporary shows, some cases are still being refused admission by hospitals. There is danger of an outbreak of epidemic disease from the influx of sick and needy persons. These tragedies are happening in an area where foodgrains at the rate of eight million lbs. a day are being delivered by two railways. This fact was revealed by the Hon'ble Sir Edward Benthall, War Transport Member, who added the influx of sick and needy persons. These tragedies are happening to all this food? It is certainly not reaching the people who need it ; that is only too tragically apparent. What has happened to Bengal's own normal stocks and crops? The province is not, a devastated war area although there have been floods and in certain district foodstocks were removed or reduced. Exports, about which Calcutta is so fond of circulating rumours, have been very small indeed. The only reasonable conclusion is that there is a supply bottleneck inside Bengal itself. In these circumstances intervention by Delhi and ruthless stamping out of supply abuses, as promised by the new Food Member, are essential in the name of suffering humanity. Fine words do not nourish starving people."

of law and order will operate ruthlessly. Is not the conflict between capitalism and democracy clear? Can the Government honestly profess concern for the welfare of the people, if it is still unable or reluctant to realise that even to-day. not yet in formal possession of power, capitalism is operating as the enemy of the people?

After the war, it will be even more so. The basic condition for post-war economic reconstruction of the world is raising the standard of living of the backward peoples. So, a very prominent place has been given to India in the scheme of post-war reconstruction. With a national-capitalist State, India will not be able to occupy that position, and make her contribution to the solution of the problems of post-war reconstruction. The established, feudal and patriarchal social relations must go if the standard of the masses of the Indian people is to be appreciably raised. It will take some time before modern industries will be able to relieve the pressure on land.[6] The peasantry constitutes the vast bulk of Indian consumers. Therefore, greater purchasing power of the peasantry is the condition for the expansion of modern industries. Indian economic life thus

---

[6] The basic problem regarding the expansion of industries in India is on occasions touched by a number of economists in the country. But it is regrettable to note that none of them, barring certain solitary exceptions, have tried to carry their ideas to their logical conclusion. *Indusritrialisation* by Dr. P. S. Lokanathan is a typical case in point. After taking a brief survey of the industrial development in the country, during the period preceding the present war, the learned Doctor writes, "But progress was far from rapid or adequate, and was mainly confined to the Consumers' Goods' Industries. Even these could not expand owing to the lack of purchasing power on the part of the large agricultural population ; thus industrialisation was in danger of coming to a halt, unless rooted in the prosperity of the rural population. The fear of over-production in the Jute, Cement, Match, Sugar and other industries became imminent." Having thus rightly diagnosed the root of the difficulty, he simply refuses to proceed to recommend the proper remedies. Quite suddenly, and surprisingly enough for the reader,

is caught in a veritable vicious circle. There is only one way out. That is to leave in the possession of the peasantry a larger share of the values produced by them. That will mean an encroachment on the privileged position of the landed aristocracy. There is no reason why capitalists should object to that measure beneficial for themselves. But in India the capitalists are very closely associated with the landed aristocracy. Therefore, in India capitalism can only be feudal capitalism, which by its very nature prefers to thrive on the economy of scarcity. Its other name is Fascism, which is denial of democracy.

Moreover, on the pretext of meeting unfair competition from abroad, Indian capitalism would insist on keeping the

---

he jumps to protection and pleads for a more fullblooded protectionist policy. (pages 8-9). One wonders what the remedy has to do with the disease as diagnosed by him. The problem, on the other hand, has been correctly stated by Dr. Radha Kamal Mukherjee, when he writes under the proper caption, 'Tariffs vs. Increase of Purchasing Power of Agriculturists as Aid to Industrialisation': "With the increase of population, the proportion of the so-called industrial workers to the total population has steadily diminished in India. Even a forward industrial policy backed by protectionism of an extreme kind can not materially alter the basic trend of India's national economy. For several decades we shall not be able to deflect more than five to seven per cent. of the total population to the big organised industries, though heavy tariffs may entail for the agricultural community an excessive burden, which of all sections in the country they can least afford to bear. . . . . On the other hand, if we continue to increase this burden by high tariffs for nourishing industrial development, we may be killing the goose that lays the golden eggs. Ireland has not been able to make much headway in the development of new industries, in spite of her newly acquired fiscal autonomy. Eire's industrial advancement has been limited by the low purchasing power of her agriculturist representing more than 75 per cent of the population, and her fiscal independence has been unable to diminish much her dependence on foreign imports of manufactures, or overcome the inherent drawbacks of her economic structure acting as a brake on her industrial development." (A Preface to Planning, page XXVII—*Economic Problems of Modern India*—edited by R. K. Mukherjee and H. L. Dey, vol. 2).

cost of production on the lowest level. Cheap labour will be the corner-stone of Indian industries built on the basis of capitalism. So, if the present Government will persist in the policy of placing Indian capitalism in the saddle, India will become the Japan of the post-war world. And as such, she will be a serious threat to all progressive plans of world reconstruction. An Indian national-capitalist State will not only prevent the rise of Indian Democracy, but will be a standing menace for world democracy. The crux of the Indian problem, therefore, is Democracy *versus* Capitalism. The British Government, which still considers itself responsible for the future of India, should therefore make no mistake in choosing sides, if it wishes to discharge its responsibility creditably.

March 21, 1943.

III

THE ABSURDITIES

In his budget speech, the Finance Member made the remark that an increase in agricultural prices meant a reduction in the burden of agricultural debt. Whether the present high price of food grains and other agricultural products is having that desired effect, still remains a controversial question. Replying to the budget debate, the Finance Member said that "such indices as are available are sufficient to satisfy us that the position of the agriculturist is definitely much better than it was before. There is no question but that a certain portion of the high prices is making its way permanently to his advantage." In course of the same debate, another Member of the Government, Sir Jogendra Singh, however, expressed a different point of view. He said that "the purchasing power does not even to-day permit a producer of food to purchase a new set of clothes for himself and his family." Then he laid down the standard—"the basic agricultural wage should cover the normal needs of an average worker regarded as a human being in a civilised State,"—which evidently has not yet been reached. The peasantry may be slightly better of to-day than previously ; but it would be a bold assertion that there is no room for their purchasing power to increase.

It is not a matter of opinion. The controversy will have to be settled with the facts of the situation, which can be ascertained. None, however, should disagree with the opinion that higher agricultural prices, provided that the benefit accrues to the peasantry, will reduce their burden of indebtedness. Further, there should be general agreement about the urgent necessity of reducing that crushing burden on the bent backs of the bulk of primary producers. Indebtedness of the peasantry has been recognised as the evil which is eating into the entire economic life of the country. Agriculture still remains the basic industry of the country. Its rationalisation, therefore, is the primary condition for any economic progress or industrial reconstruction. Readiness to face and solve that basic problem should not be wanting when there is so much talk about post-war reconstruction.

In its memorable report on the problem of post-war reconstruction, the London Chamber of Commerce has indicated the following approach to that problem: "It is now essential, if greater disasters are to be avoided, so to change the system as to ensure that international trade shall tend to raise the standard of living of the backward nations to that of the advanced nations." Nevertheless, the British commercial community in this country does not seem to have as yet grasped the problem, and is therefore not able to realise the "absurdities" of an antiquated economic system so graphically depicted and roundly condemned by the London Chamber of Commerce.

The leader of the European Group in the Central Legislative Assembly disagreed with the view of the Finance Member, and warned against "the dangers inherent in increased purchasing power due to inflation." If the report is true, then Sir Henry Richardson gave yet another evidence of the absurdities of a system which he is so very anxious to maintain, even at the cost of the interest he is supposed to represent. Let alone the question of agricultural indebtedness, the plight of the Indian peasantry may not be a matter of concern for the European businessmen living in cities. But as businessmen, they should know that, if the Indian peasants can buy more, businessmen will be able to sell more; and that after all is the concern not only of traders, but of industrialists. Industries cannot prosper if trade is restricted by low purchasing power of the bulk of the consumers.

So very absurd was the position taken up by the leader of the European commercial community, that it provoked the following retort from Sir Jogendra Singh: "May I begin by mentioning that even in normal years our (agricultural) production is not sufficient to give all the people a balanced diet, and the purchasing power which frightens Sir Henry Richardson does not even to-day permit a producer of food to purchase a new set of clothes for himself and his family? The emphasis on dangers which lurk in an increased purchasing power, coming from a leader of the British mercantile community, strikes a note which recalls to my mind the words of a Persian poet who exclaimed: 'When heresy springs from Kaba itself, where can faith abide'?"

Sir Jogendra Singh's poetic retort emphasises the absurdities of an economic system which may have been useful in the past, but have now become antagonistic even to trade and industry. But the European commercial community in this country is not yet prepared to agree with the London Chamber of Commerce that "there is something radically wrong with our economic system." And therefore it cannot realise that "it is absurd that men in want of the necessaries of life should be denied the money with which to buy them." Sir Henry Richardson is afraid of letting the Indian peasantry have a little more money, because that can be done only by allowing the price of agricultural commodities to rise. As a businessman, he should be able to see without any difficulty that more money in the hand of the peasantry will be a great impetus to trade. But he is obsessed with a more immediate concern which can be characterised as short-sighted self-interest. If the price of food grains, which constitute the bulk of Indian agricultural product, go up, industrial employers will have to pay higher wages, not as a matter of charity, but in order to prevent deterioration of labour, owing to insufficient nutrition. They are fighting shy of raising real wages, *for their own interest,* and are trying the make-shift arrangement of granting generally inadequate dearness allowance. If the agricultural prices are stabilised on a higher level for larger economic considerations, the question of raising real wages of industrial labour must be eventually faced. That question seems to be haunting the commercial community.

This mentality makes all the talk about post-war reconstruction not only meaningless, but ridiculous. It assumes that cheap labour must always remain the foundation of industry in this country. In order to keep the price of labour on the lowest possible level, the general standard of living must remain below the civilised standard. That is the fundamental feature of what is called colonial economy,—a system of trade built on the basis of surplus capital exported from industrially advanced countries, and consequently getting the backward countries into unpayable indebtedness. The London Chamber of Commerce has condemned that system as one of the absurdities of the nineteenth century economic system which assumed that "the only proper object of an economic system was to produce the maximum of real wealth with the minimum of labour, and therefore looked to division of labour, carried to its extreme limit, not only as between people within the nation, but as between one nation and another."

We have characterised that bold pronouncement as a condemnation of Imperialism. Nor is it a matter of inference. The Report of the London Chamber of Commerce is more outspoken: "It was palpably absurd that nations should be desperately anxious to export more of their real wealth to other nations than they received in return."

If the export of capital, to get the backward countries into unpayable indebtedness, was absurd, it must be abandoned once it has been discovered as such. Consequently, the structure of Indian economy must change. It must cease to be colonial economy. It must seek another, more stable, basis than cheap labour. The British commercial community in this country does not seem to have realised that as yet. But how long will they ignore the fact that the ground has been cut under the system of colonial economy which they would still like to retain? After the war, the surplus of India's export trade, carried on by British firms, will be balanced by importing commodities. It will no longer be available as capital to be invested in India. The London Chamber of Commerce has accepted that as a principle to guide international trade after the war. Consequently, to increase the purchasing power of India, will be to the interest of the British commercial community. Otherwise, India will not be able to accept increased imports to balance her surplus export.

That change in India's foreign trade will be a determining factor in her post-war reconstruction. But until now, all talks about post-war reconstruction have been rather vague. As a matter of fact, it is a rather loose notion. For India, there will be no reconstruction. India has suffered very little from the war, unlike other belligerent countries. Consequently, there will be nothing to reconstruct. It will be a process of construction—from the bottom up. The problem will be how to remove the absurdities which have been created by capitalism prospering under the war conditions.

In all countries, modern industries developed on the basis of the capitalist mode of production. Imperialism prevented that development in India. As a matter of fact, it did not prevent the growth of capitalism ; under colonial economy, capitalism could not function as a progressive force. Now Imperialism is removing itself. Colonial economy, therefore, should also go. What can be called feudal capitalism is the characteristic feature of colonial economy. The essence of feudalism, whatever may be its superstructure, either agrarian or industrial, is to deprive the direct producer of his entire surplus product. Consequently, the vast bulk of the population remains on a very low standard of living. Unless Indian economic life will be freed from that stagnation, no construction will be possible.

Is there any ground to assume that, on the disappearance of Imperialism, capitalism will operate in India as a progressive factor? For the welfare of her own people, as well as to make her contribution to the post-war reconstruction of the rest of the world, India must become a modern, prosperous, progressive, civilised country. Is that possible within the limits of capitalism? In other words, is it possible for capitalism to be free in India of those absurdities which are its characteristic feature once the system becomes antiquated? These are questions which must be answered by those who propose to make any practical plan for the construction of India's economic life on the basis of modern industries. On no other basis is it possible to rationalise the economic life of the country. Those are not theoretical questions. They arise from the faults of the situation, and therefore should be answered having due regard for the facts, as they are to-day, and as they are going to be in the post-war world.

No plan of reconstruction will meet the realities of the Indian situation, unless it is a plan of large-scale industrialisation. The success of the plan will depend on three conditions: supply of labour, abundance of capital, and market. The first two conditions are evidently there.

The basic cause of the economic backwardness of India is the fact that the vast bulk of her labour supply is not fruitfully employed. It is practically wasted. Therefore, Indian industries will have a greater supply of labour than it will be able to cope with in the beginning. Nor will there be any lack of capital. Apart from fluid capital, there is a large store of accumulated wealth which can be easily converted into productive capital. Moreover, India is already experiencing the absurdity of possessing a growingly large credit with which she does not know what to do. It is the sterling balances piling up in London. This absurdity will lead to yet another absurdity if international trade will not be reformed according to the principles of "A Twentieth Century Economic System" recommended by the London Chamber of Commerce. The new absurdity will arise out of the refusal of Indian capitalists to accept payment from Britain in goods. If after the war India's destiny will be in the hands of the national capitalists, the sterling balance piling up in London to her credit will be a veritable embarrassment of riches. Nevertheless, they are already making their irrational influence felt. They have compelled the Finance Member to withdraw the proposal that a reconstruction fund should be created out of the sterling balances. Something, however, must be done with the money. The credit may be transferred to some other country. But in any case, in order to derive any benefit from it, India will have to import goods either from Britain or from any other country of her choice. Most probably, in order to avoid competition, consumers' goods will not be accepted. But capital goods cannot be imported except in connection with a plan of industrialisation. As a matter of fact, the Finance Member has given a rather broad hint that the sterling balances will have to be used in payment of the capital goods which India will need after the war. So, the second condition for an industrialisation of the country is already there.

Only the third condition still remains problematical, and that after all is the decisive condition. With the two conditions, commodities could be produced almost without limit. But they must be sold. Where is the market? Evidently, that question should also create no difficulty. A country with a population of more than four hundred millions, and still growing rapidly, presents an inexhaustible market. But at present, it is only a potential market. The human demand is there. How to transform the human demand into effective demand? That is the fundamental problem of Indian reconstruction. The debate referred to in the beginning of this article shows that this problem cannot be solved within the limits of orthodox capitalism—that is, limitation of production to the existing demand, disregarding human demand.

In order to raise the standard of living of the bulk of

the population, the feudal character of national economy must go. In a certain stage of history, capitalism operates as a progressive factor precisely because it frees society from the bonds of feudal economy. Therefore, if in India capitalism cannot raise the standard of living of the bulk of the population, it will create only new absurdities. One of them will be to raise the bogey of inflation in order to keep agricultural prices as well as wages low. That is already being done. On the one hand, Indian capitalists are complaining against inflation, and British commercial community is haunted by the imaginary danger of a high agricultural price. Between the two, they will create absurdities galore, and bedevil any plan of Indian reconstruction.

The alternative is not a headlong advance towards Socialism. It is planned production, according to needs, and the realisation that trade has no other function than free exchange of commodities. All the three factors for India becoming a prosperous country herself, and contributing to the reconstruction of the world, are there. An economic system which would not permit the freest use of those factors is evidently anti-social, and as such should be discarded. Capitalism must be judged by that standard. The plan of Indian reconstruction should also be made according to that standard.

March 28, 1943.

IV

AXIS OF INDIAN POLITICS

The Government of India, through the Secretary of State, is constitutionally responsible to the British Parliament, which represents British Democracy. So, ultimately, the latter is responsible for the governance of India. But the British people has no more to do with Indian politics than the people of this country. If they had, the present Government of India would not be allowed to pursue the policy of persistently ignoring Indian Democracy and placating the upper classes even when the political spokesmen of these latter are in open revolt against the Government.

Indian politics is determined by Britishers having a stake in this country, together with the native upper classes who are steadily gaining preponderance, thanks to the emergency conditions created by the war. The relation between imperialist capital and national capitalism has changed so much that the latter is suggesitng transfer of British investments in this country to Indians in payment of the war supplies purchased by the Government. Investments made through loans raised by the Government of India in London have already been so transferred very largely. A considerable part of private British capital directly invested has also changed hands. So much so that the head of a powerful British business organisation in this country is reported to have remarked recently that his organisation was making money to be distributed as dividends to the Marwaris. Something must be rescued out of the ruins ; Commission Agents' fees are quite handsome. Therefore, British businessmen, even those who have been reduced to the status of Commission Agents, are very anxious to cultivate friendly relations with Indian vested interests, hoping that the latter may be persuaded not to take up a monopolistic attitude. Moreover, it is hoped that India under a capitalist government, even if the predominating position may have to be conceded to the native capitalists, will provide a refuge for British capital fleeing from Britain menaced by the spectre of Socialism. That provides the basis for an alliance of vested interests—foreign and native ; and that alliance already formed is the axis of Indian politics.

The government of the country is controlled by the alliance. A government not only administers the country ; it also can and actually does influence the politics of the country, including the position of parties and individuals opposed to itself. Without the anxiety of the imperialist government to come to terms with the native upper classes constituting the social basis of nationalism, the Congress could not attain the position where it became a thorn in the side of the Government. Political representation was always followed by economic concessions to the upper classes ; and economic concessions to the patrons of nationalist politics only whetted its appetite and encouraged it to defy repression. Then, except in the case of avowed revolutionaries and terrorists, political repression was always half-hearted. The Government was always eager to come to terms with the Congress and other upper-class nationalist leaders. Even to-day, power may be handed over to them if their dictator would only assure his noble friend at New Delhi that he was sorry for what has taken place since August last year. Even after putting them under comfortable preventive arrest, the Government is anxious not to do anything which might undermine their political position. While in office in the provinces, Congress leaders gave all satisfaction to vested interests, British as well as Indian. Therefore, the British businessmen also want that, should power be transferred to Indian hands, Congressmen should be preferred to others. The present rulers of the country, who individually are naturally influenced by the opinion of British businessmen, therefore, are so very reluctant to discredit the heir-designate, even when the latter is to be kept under some restraint for the time being.

The political organisation of the country (the State) is buttressed on economic relations which, in their turn, are defended by the State. That is the object of law and order. Law means protection of property, and order is the established economic order which deprives the producing masses of most of the fruits of their labour.

The alliance of vested interests is the most predominating economic relation constituting the basis of the present Government. Therefore, that alliance is the axis of Indian politics as a whole.

The latest move to protect the interests of the alliance is the plan of "immobilising purchasing power".[1] The

---

[1] It is significant to note what the representative of the Bombay Millowners said in this connection in the Central Legislative Assembly. Referring to the vexed question of inflation, Sir Vitthal Chandavarkar said, "Some of the remedies which I have suggested—limitation of cash bonuses, limitation of cash dearness allowances, limitation of cash payments, will I think have some effects in checking the prices of commodities." He also observed, "I am not speaking of limitation of dividends. But indirectly this policy might also result in the limitation of dividends. A direct limitation of dividends may be resented and may not be in the interests of the industries." With reference to this proposal, Sir Jeremy Raisman said, "I am very interested in the what he said about the question of compulsory savings. . . But I understood Sir Vitthal Chandavarkar to deprecate an approach to this matter by way of a restriction of dividends. I find that rather difficult to reconcile or to understand. In my opinion, the action to be taken

necessity for this arises only when there is more money than the people need for purchasing their requirements. And it is now a generally accepted maxim of sociology that there should be no arbitrary limit to the requirements of the civilised human being. If is a notorious fact that the vast bulk of the Indian people, nearly ninety per cent., do not have their most minimum requirements adequately satisfied. Therefore, a very considerable amount of money will have to go in their pockets before the necessity of immobilising their purchasing power will at all arise. How, then, does this absurd idea enter the heads of the rulers of this country?

The necessity of purchasing war supplies in this country has caused a considerable expansion of currency. That is taken as the evidence of increased purchasing power of the people. Before planning any restriction of spending by the masses, one should find out what portion of the newly created money has actually found its way to them. The net result of the expansion of currency has not been increased purchasing power on the part of the masses, but to force up prices of food stuffs and other primary commodities to a high level inaccessible to their purchasing capacity. That is the most oustanding fact of the present economic situation and it can be ignored only with consummate deliberation. If the prices were kept anywhere near the pre-war level by energetic Government intervention, then there might be some

---

on this front must include action in relation to dividends as well as to bonuses, and all other forms in which increased purchasing power is handed out, whether to the employing classes or the investing classes or labour.

Sir Vitthal Chandavarkar: Again I said my proposal would lead to the restriction of dividends and to that extent it would achieve both the objects.

Sir Jeremy Raisman: It seems to me that it may be that the most practical approach to this matter would be by restriction of dividends accompanied by a provision for compulsory savings.

surplus money in the possession of the masses. The possibility of increased supply for civil consumption being restricted by war emergency, the surplus could then be immobilised through obligatory saving or some other device. But to compel the people to spend less when they cannot buy enough to eat even with their hypothetically increased income, is simply to condemn them to starvation. No sensible government would launch upon such a policy which, given the political atmosphere of the country, might be suicidal for itself.

But most probably, against the better judgment of at least some of its members, the Government is compelled to adopt this suicidal policy under the pressure of the alliance of vested interests which dominates Indian politics. The absurd plan of immobilising the purchasing power of the masses, absurd because their increased purchasing power is a fiction, on the plea of currency inflation, has no other object than to pass on the burden of financing the war on the already bent back of the poor people. The latter having no place in the scheme of Indian politics, cannot oppose the plan, but, being easily swayed by nationalist propaganda, may be driven by additional hardships to desperate actions. To meet that eventuality, the Government will set the machine of law and order in motion. But how will it justify the sacrifice of Indian Democracy to satisfy the insatiable greed of vested interests? Ultimately, account will have to be rendered to British Democracy.

Let us have a closer look at the scare-crow of inflation. On the top, it is a credit expansion, which is entirely different from inflationary practice. The Government does not pay either in cash or in currency notes. The usual medium of payment for government purchases is cheque or other forms of bank credit. Currency expansion has been much less.[2] So, the real position is that the currency expansion has been caused by higher prices which are purely speculative and profiteering. It has not forced up prices, as generally maintained. Therefore, it is not inflation.

The second point to be noted is that only a small part of money paid to the middlemen filters down to the primary producer. That is evident from the disparity between the expansion of currency and the rise of wholesale prices. While the former is about 250 p.c., the latter is less than a hundred p. c. The price paid to the primary producers is much lower than the price in the wholesale market. Therefore, a very small fraction of the additional currency issued for war purchases is in circulation among the masses of the people. The *per capita* incidence would be hardly one rupee. In view of the enormous rise in retail prices paid by the consumers, that is a negligible increase in their purchasing power. And if even that is immobilised, there will be very little contraction of currency, although it will mean additional hardship for the people.

The great bulk of currency put in circulation for the purchase of war supplies thus has accumulated in the posses-

---

[2] It is interesting that this aspect of currency expansion should have escaped the attention of most of our academic writers who have been all along clamouring against inflation. A significant exception is Prof. D. Ghosh. He writes, "We can, however, do much in respect of our net receipts from the British Government. The size of these receipts depends on the amount of real goods and services we handle on behalf of the U.K. and the prices we pay for them. We can not alter the former which is determined by the necessities of the war ; but we can significantly control the latter and thereby reduce the money value of our receipts. The more effectively we regulate prices and costs and the more carefully the Supply Department makes its purchases, the smaller will be the inflow of new money from outside." (D. Ghosh: *War and the Rupee,* page 12.)

sion of traders and government contractors.[3] Larger fortunes made by bigger businessmen remain in the form of credit and capital investment. Those who hold the bulk of war-time currency cannot possibly use even a small fraction of it for the purpose of consumption. There is the increased purchasing power to be immobilised, and the immobilisation can effectively take place through economically sounder methods than obligatory saving.

Too much liquid money in the possession of the trading class is now used for hoarding food grains and other primary necessities for profiteering and speculative purposes. How else can they use the money? Bank rates are very low. The interest on Government Securities or War Loans is higher, but does not satisfy those who have tested blood and want to get richer quickly. A *plethora* of money in the possession of the non-producing trading class has given birth to the evils of hoarding ad profiteering. Therefore, the Government's repeatedly declared desire to combat those evils cannot materialise unless a rigorous system of control—not only of prices but of stocks—is introduced. But the alliance which constitutes the axis of Indian politics, and dominates the policy of the Government, has prevented the latter from doing the most obvious, that which will immediately lay this bogey of inflation, and incidentally relieve the economic distress of the people.

---

[3] The following are the figures for the war contracts during the last three years:

Rs.	78.7 Crores	1940-41
,,	184 ,,	1941-42
,,	256.6 ,,	1942-43

The total figure since the beginning of the war to the 31st of March 1943, is 548 crores of Rupees. The purchases from the small scale industries were in 1941-42 Rs. 5 crores and in 1942-43 Rs. 10 crores. (Reserve Bank of India: *Report on Currency and Finance* for 1942-43, page 11.)

What is needed to stabilise the economic life of the country is to prevent liquid money accumulating in the possession of the non-productive trading class. That can be done in two ways: First, by bringing the price actually paid to the primary producer up to the level of the wholesale price, which is paid by the Government purchasing war supplies. The resulting rise in the cost of living of the urban population, particularly the industrial workers, should be counter-balanced by higher wages. There will follow an even distribution of money, and the necessary expansion of currency will lose its inflationary character, if it really possesses. it.[4]

[4] Much confusion seems to prevail on this point. It is often argued from various quarters that inflation can be checked by borrowing and taxation. The statement issued by leading economists in the country also insists on this method. "We earnestly feel that immediate and drastic measures to check inflation are called for. In this connection we urge on the Government the primary necessity of closing the 'gap' by increased taxation and borrowing." (Manifesto by Indian Economists on the recent economic policy of the Government of India, published on April, 12, 1943: *Financial Burden of the War on India* by C. N. Vakil, page 135.) The same remedy has also been suggested by Prof. C. N. Vakil, Dr. G. R. Gadgil and several others. Certain observations from the publication of Prof. D. Ghosh are however significant and noteworthy in this connection. He writes, "If new money is flowing in from outside and the tide can not be stemmed wholly, the instrument of public finance should be used to put that new money out of harm's way. The Government should take away from the public by means of taxation and borrowing larger sums than it requires for current expenditure and impound the surplus into some suspense account; or if excess money is left in the hands of the public, measures should be adopted to make it unspendable. Moreover the scale and the method of transfer should be such that the former is induced or compelled to draw upon its active balance; a mere transfer into Government accounts of money, that would have otherwise lain idle with the public, does not alter total spending or depress prices. From this point of view, taxation is superior to borrowing. For when a man pays taxes, he feels poorer, and tries to adjust by cutting down his current expenditure. But when he subscribes to a loan he merely exchanges one asset—unconsumed money income—into another, in this case, Government of India securities. He does not feel poorer and he does not reduce his expenses in the

The other way is to make a large part of the payment for war purchases in credit, which should be frozen for the duration of the war to prevent speculative dealings.[5] That will create a guarantee against the possible danger of inflation without committing the suicidal act of depressing the

---

present. Secondly, we should rely less on indirect taxes or consumption taxes ; these restrict real consumption but do not necessarily reduce total spending. Thirdly, the scheme of taxation should impinge more on active than on idle balances. On this principle, small incomes should be taxed heavily than the large ; for the former contain more than propotionately smaller idle balances. But the obvious inequity of this idea suggests that in the case of smaller incomes, we should aim at postponement of present use rather than taxation as the means of reducing current spending. (*War and Rupee,* pages 18-19.) And again, "Before we can think of taxation small incomes effectively, we must guarantee stable prices and provide safeguards against a greater reduction of real incomes in the present than is consciously aimed at. We must in other words control prices and ration supplies of essential commodities properly ; before we can legitimately ask the person with a small income to postpone enjoyment or use of any portion of it. It is our failure in the field of price-control and regulated distribution of goods which seriously curtails our opportunity to make use of other methods of fighting inflation. (*War and the Rupee,* pages 23-24.)

[5] Sir Vitthal Chandavarkar, representative of the Bombay Millowners, speaking in the Central Legislative Assembly, said, "One thing has to be confessed that the people are not inclined to put money in Government loans. Even industrial concerns which formerly used to invest their money in Government loans are buying industrial shares even at the present prices ; and the reduction in he post office accounts—what does it show? It shows first that the people have no confidence in the Government and are not behind the war effort. There is no doubt it is a very unfortunate situation ; as far as I am concerned. I regret very much indeed that a large number of people are not supporting Government loans. They are deliberately not investing in the Government securities and are persuading people not to buy defence loans." Of course we can not share Sir Vitthal's broadmindedness in identifying the small section of the community, capable of investing funds in the Government loans with the people in the country. But the statement throws a flood of light on how this section has all along attempted to 'strike' in the midst of a dangerous situation. This is also an important factor accounting for the expansion of currency in the country to-day.

already low purchasing power of the masses. Every economist knows that it is a suicidal act, particularly in a country where extremely low standard of living of the bulk of the population sets a decisive limit to the economic development of the country. Production comes before distribution. If distribution is so devised as to check production, the entire economic life will be stultified.

At present, currency notes in circulation amount to slightly above 400 crores of rupees. If the entire amount is distributed according to the first suggestion, additional money in the possession of the primary producer will be considerably less than a rupee per capita (including children and all other non-producing dependants). Indeed, the incidence of increased purchasing power will be much less, because quite a substantial portion of the currency must still remain higher up for commercial transactions.

Such a slight increase of purchasing power cannot possibly have an inflationary effect. It will be more than counter-balanced by higher prices of manufactured goods.

Nevertheless, even to-day, when the increased purchasing power of the primary producer is a mere fiction, the larger portion of additional currency remaining in possession of the trading classes to be used for speculative purposes, the Government is planning to immobilise increased purchasing power. The object of the plan is to shift the burden of financing the war to the dumb millions whose voice is heard neither in nationalist politics nor in Government policy, the latter being determined exclusively by the alliance of Indian and British vested interests, which constitute the axis of Indian politics.

But it is going to be a suicidal plan. Greater purchasing power, very much greater than can possibly result from letting the primary producers have their share of the benefit of war time currency expansion, will alone guarantee against a post-war slump, which seems to be haunting businessmen, British as well as Indian, like a nightmare. Instead of an economy of plenty, they want an economy of scarcity, even when plentiful production and consumption are possible.[6] In order to provide the Indian people with the most elementary physical necessities, the productive apparatus of the country can be increased many-manifold.[7] Therefore, it is idle to contend that, if industries expanded too much during the war, there would be over-production when after the war they will have to be shifted to the production of consumers' goods.

Fascism is the politics of the economy of scarcity. Therefore, the axis of Indian politics must be broken if vic-

---

[6] "Despite a plethora of investable funds and an absence of restrictions on new capital issues, the number of new companies floated in the last three years is less than in the three preceding peace years. Only existing companies increased their activity." (*Industrialisation* by P. S. Lokanathan, p. 16.)

[7] The following from the speech of the late Governor of The Reserve Bank of India, Sir James Taylor, at the annual general meeting of the shareholders of the Bank (August, 10, 1942) is particularly significant in this connection: "As regards the former, I dislike the term inflation which, as popularly interpreted, often confuses cause and effect, as meaning a general rise in prices, caused by avoidable expansion of currency. Though there has been a considerable rise in prices in India, I do not consider that this is the result of the increase in the currency, but rather that the two phenomena together are the unavoidable result of the large purchases of goods and services being made by the British Government, for which they give us sterling which we exchange for rupees. Unless this increase in purchasing power can be met by an equal increase in the supply, not only of the articles being directly purchased by the Government, but also of the foodstuffs and other necessaries of life which those who are producing these supplies require to keep them going, and which they are now in a position to purchase owing to the money now accruing to them, there is bound to be an increase in the commodity prices in this country." Mr. G. D. Birla quoting the observation poses the question in a

tory in this was is not to make India a home of Fascism. That is necessary as much for the welfare of the Indian people as for that of the British people. An economy of scarcity may head off a slump in India. But it will have the contrary effect on British industries, which will find it very difficult to do without the Indian market. But the dictators of Indian politics want to contract the market for their immediate gain, and the Government responsible to British Democracy and claiming to be the trustee of the Indian people gives in, thereby betraying its constitutional responsibility as well as moral trust.

An Anglo-British democratic alliance can alone break the axis of Indian politics. The present Government of India is constitutionally responsible to British Democracy. It would betray the responsibility if they continue to be dictated by the reactionary alliance constituting the axis

---

still more categorical manner: "How on earth a reduction in the note circulation from 590 crores to 179 crores can possibly mean more cloth, more food, more salt, more kerosene, more cement or more wood? How, if one fine morning the Government decide to withdraw 400 crores of notes from circulation (and it could be done by various injurious methods like heavy taxation and heavy borrowing) will that eliminate the distressful sight of long queues waiting for hours before grain shops to get a few seers of wheat? How can this simple measure of cancelling a few hundred crores worth of notes create an affluence of all goods? Not even the most learned in such matters can tell us how. You may arbitrarily reduce prices, tax people so as to drain off the last drop of their blood. You can not create more goods unless either you produce them, or His Majesty's Government and other Allied nations stop drawing on Indian goods for their needs. Of course we can always create an influence by imposing dyspepsia on consumers if that be something desirable. Else, in order to meet the situation we must produce more. There is no getting away from this simple fact." (*Inflation or Scarcity.*) It is, however, significant that Mr. Birla forgets to refer to the following sentence that appears in the speech of Sir James Taylor: "We also have the hoarder and the speculator always with us, the people who hoard either so that they may not go short themselves on in the hope of reselling at a profit later."

of Indian politics. The only constitutional thing for it to do, in the given situation, is to help the rise of Indian Democracy, and thus further the formation of the Indo-British Democratic Alliance, to guarantee post-war reconstruction of both the countries on such a line as will promote the larger interests of the two.

June 6, 1943.

V

BROTHERHOOD OF BIG BUSINESS

The financial policy of the Government of India has always been criticised and opposed by Indian big business and its political spokesmen inside and outside Legislative Assemblies. Recently, the opposition has taken the form of attack upon the method of financing war purchases. It is condemned as inflation which will ruin Indian business. Some go to the extent of maintaining that the present financial policy of the Government is meant to have that effect. We have already discussed whether currency expansion necessitated by the requirements of the war is inflation or not. We shall investigate the matter still further. But whether it means inflation or not, the fact remains that the result of war time currency expansion has been entirely favourable for Indian business. Indeed, without it the latter could not enjoy the war time boom. Nor is the advantage going to be temporary, to disappear after the war. The entire financial relation between Britain and India has changed, to the advantage of the latter. As far as big business is concerned, India has advanced a long way towards decolonisation. British big business, of course, still remains in this country. But its financially monopolist position has been irreparably shaken. The Government policy of financing the war having thus entirely benefited Indian big business, its opposition to that policy is evidently politically motivated. Indian big business is aspiring for the monopolist position.

There is a Sanskrit proverb that, when a wise man is threatened with the loss of everything, he voluntarily sacrifices half in order to save the other half. The British businessmen in this country seem to have reconciled themselves to the unfavourable consequences of the war, and are eager to act according to the old wisdom. They want to enter into a partnership with Indian big business, even on the latter's terms. The projected brotherhood of big business would be the Mentor of India's destiny. But all its plans will be frustrated if it disregards the other wise old dictum. Don't kill the goose that lays the golden eggs. The danger of the plan being miscarried need not worry those who are concerned with the economic prosperity of the Indian people. But the attempt to execute the shortsighted plan of the brotherhood of big business will aggravate the hardships of the Indian people. Therefore, the plan must be opposed and the most effective opposition will be to expose its fallacies.

Firstly, let us show that Indian big business has no reason to complain against the financial policy of the Government of India. If it were concerned with the promotion of the economic welfare of the country as a whole, to-day it is in a position to do so. Economic progress of the country is conditional upon expansion of modern industry. The creation of that condition was retarded by two factors: low purchasing power of the Indian masses and the control of India's economic life by British finance. The war time boom should now enable Indian big business to distribute more purchasing power to the masses and thus create the primary condition for a rapid expansion of modern industry. But Indian big business attached the greatest importance to fiscal autonomy. It maintained that without fiscal autonomy, economic progress of India was not possible. Now it has attained complete fiscal autonomy.

In consequence of this war, India has become a creditor

of England. In 1936 the Government of India's sterling debt amounted to 360 million pound. It is now estimated that by the end of this year the indebtedness will be reduced to 12 million pound. As against that almost complete disappearance of India's indebtedness to Britain, to-day there is a sterling balance of several hundred millions to her favour in London. India has attained this highly advantageous financial position thanks to the efforts of her "imperialist" government, which negotiated with the British Treasury regarding the division of defence expenditure in a manner as if India was semi-neutral in this war. That was a tremendous concession to Indian big business.[1] The concession was made in the critical days when Indian big business was tempted by the Axis offer of an advantageous partnership. The political spokesmen of Indian big business

[1] "The persistent accumulation of sterling in favour of India and the consequent ability of that country to repatriate between March 1936 and January 1943, of £284,000,000 out of £376,000,000 of sterling debt will cause less astonishment in the light of information given this week in New Delhi about the financial relation between the United Kingdom and the Indian Governments. Sir Jeremy Raisman, the Finance Member, speaking in the Assembly on his return from a financial mission to London, announced that the following expenditure in respect of supply and defence incurred in India had been made chargeable to the U. K. Government.

1939-40	actual	Rs. 4 crores.	(£ 3000000.)
1940-41	actual	Rs. 53 crores.	(£40000000.)
1941-42	Revised Estimates	Rs. 185 crores.	(£14000000.)
1942-43	Budgeted	Rs. 387 crores.	(£29000000.)

This is in addition to free supplies of war materials by this country estimated at £45000000 for the current financial year, and to increasing Lend-Lease aid from United States. Moreover, no part of the expenditure incurred by using Indian troops outside India, has been or will be debited to Indian Revenue. With these heavy sterling grants to reinforce the considerable favourable balance of payments caused by the war, sufficient explanation is provided of the substantial net sterling income from which India has benifited since the beginning of the war." (*The Economist,* September, 26, 1942. p. 393.)

were opposed to India participating in this war and, given the opportunity, might have preferred to remain neutral as a gesture of response to the Axis offer. To treat Indian big business *de facto* as a semi-neutral was a counter move of the Government. India was not expected to make any more contribution to the war than to sell goods and services, and big business was given the freedom to charge fancy prices for the goods supplied. This was one bird delivered by Britain to the hand of Indian big business as against two in the bush promised by the Axis Powers. The political nature of the financial deal is evident. But it did not quite serve the political purpose. Exacting its pound of flesh from the British Government in distress, Indian big business continued to patronise and finance the "Quit India" movement of the Congress which could only please the Axis Powers. Financial bribe did not end the political danger. Ultimately, the danger had to be combated with more straightforward methods and appropriate weapons. As far as the receivers of the financial concession were concerned, their appetite was whetted up. They wanted more and more. To-day they are in a position to dictate terms to British big business on the threat of outright expropriation or eventual expulsion from the country. A National Government controlled by Indian big business will be the instrument to implement both those threats. Therefore, Indian big business is not satisfied with its virtual dictatorship, but is pressing for formal political power. British big business wants to be on the winning side, even as a junior partner of the brotherhood of big business.

A few more figures to illustrate the present position. The interest charges of the Government of India's sterling debt amounted to 46 crores of rupees before the war. The debts have not been cancelled. They have been repatriated to India. That means, bonds held in London have been transferred to India. The purpose of the transaction was to enable the British Government to pay off a part of its obligations to the Government of India on account of war purchases made in this country. The purchases were made from Indian businessmen. The payment was made to them. So, the bonds are held by them to-day. 46 crores of rupees a year previously paid to British investors will be paid to them from now on. To that extent, the Government of India comes under their financial control. The Finance Member of the Government of India described the situation as follows. "The real gain to the country lies in the liquidation of external obligations, and their replacement by internal debt." The Imperialist Government of India had been put in chains of gold—by Indian big business. The chain is much heavier than the repatriated sterling debt. The sterling balances to India's favour at present amount to well over 500 crores of rupees. The British Government owes that much to the Government of India. And that represents the liability of the Government of India for purchases made from Indian businessmen.

The financial relation between the Indian and British business community inside India is also changing. Indian business are investing the money they are making out of the war. They are buying up shares in companies previously with predominating British interests. Consequently, Indian finance has acquired controlling position in the coal, jute and tea industries. With a similar or even stronger position in the textile, iron and steel, cement and sugar industries, they can now easily dominate the entire economic life of the country.

Indian big business has acquired this predominating position entirely thanks to the British Government purchasing war supplies in this country. The supplies had to be paid for. The medium of payment had to be created. Currency expansion, therefore, was unavoidable. It is idle for Indian big business to complain of inflation, which has so far been only to their advantage.

For the Government, the expansion of currency was unavoidable. War supplies were urgently needed. They were not to be had free; and the Imperialist Government was too considerate of Indian vested interest to tax war profiteers heavily.[2] Therefore, the Government had to defend its financial policy against the charge of inflation. But of late it has suddenly changed its front, and joined the chorus against the bogey of inflation. British big business, of course, has all along been apprehensive of the bogey. So, now the brotherhood of big business can be formed under official patronage. It is a united front against the Indian people. And it is formed with the incredibly stupid purpose of killing the goose which might lay golden eggs if it was properly taken care of. The goose is the Indian consuming masses. At present, it is much too starved to lay any eggs. But, it is of the kind which does lay golden eggs when it is properly kept and fed. The United front will ultimately repent its stupid greed. But, in the meantime, it will cause greater hardship to the Indian people.

Let us now look at the bogey of inflation. It is one of those financial mystifications about which nobody has ever written anything intelligibly.[3] Among the high-priests of

---

[2] "The profits from war industries today are, in many cases said to be such as to pay for the entire capital equipment in a year or two, notwithstanding the income and the super taxes and the excess profits duty." (*How India pays for the War* by K. T. Shah p. 52.)

[3] Apart from its ironical tone, the following which occurs in an article in *The Eastern Economist* is highly interesting, "And to

public finance, there is no agreement about what constitutes inflation.[4] There are divergent theories. The generally accepted and easily understandable theory is that it is inflation to issue currency notes not sufficiently covered by gold or other securities. On that token, there is no inflation in India.[5] The note issue is covered by the gold held by the

---

my bewilderment as the controversy proceeded and as the literature on inflation continued to inflate I learnt that there is not one kind of inflation but several: credit inflation, monetary infiation, price inflation, deficit-induced inflation, Sterling-seduced inflation, fiat-money inflation, illusory inflation, galloping inflation, cantering inflation, consumptive inflation, invisible inflation, defrauding inflation, inflation which is concealed taxation, and last but not the least, inflation which is not inflation at all but expansion accompanied by scarcity." (July 30, 1943. page 384.)

[4] While the facts relating to the expansion of currency in India are indeed inconvertible and must be studied closely, this labelling of those facts is indeed meaningless and absurd. It is generally done on the basis of Prof. Irving Fisher's Equation of Exchange. It is however widely known that Prof. Fisher's formulation is not acceptable to a number of other important authorities, like Prof. Pigou. Dr. Keynes has distinguished between three types of inflation: commodity inflation, income inflation and profits inflation. There are others who hold the view that inflation has nothing to do with either currency or prices. It may accompany a constant, an increasing or a decreasing quantity of money, or stable, rising or falling prices. These various views occasionally overlap and often contradict each other.

[5] "Have we really inflation here? . . . I would not go into the nicety of the distinction between the terms 'inflation' and 'expansion'. One wonders whether in view of the bad odour of the word Inflation, as it came to prevail in postwar Russia and Germany, it would not be more appropriate to call the increased circulation in our case by the term expansion. Our issue is fully covered by sterling, the purchasing power of which has not so far depreciated." (G. D. Birla—*Inflation or Scarcity?*) Mr. Birla further goes on to assert that nothing can alter the "fact that sterling at present is solvent and our currency at the moment does not lack an adequate backing. To call this position inflation may lead people into believing that like the German mark or the Russian rouble the rupee has gone insolvent which it certainly has not." The following observations from an article by Mr. L. Nemenyi, Foreign Expert to the Central Banking Inquiry Committee (1930) are also noteworthy in this connection: "Typical characteristics of inflation are an enormous rise in the circulation of notes backed purely by

Reserve Bank of India plus rupee securities and finally the sterling securities piling up in London. According to the most orthodox theoreticians, the Government of India is entitled to issue several times more notes than in circulation on the basis of the assets held by the Reserve Bank. Since the beginning of the war the note circulation has increased by about 250 p.c. India's sterling balances in London alone have increased by nearly 600 p.c. during the same period.

Evidently, the expansion of currency has not been inflationary. Notes had to be issued to pay for war supplies. The only plausible argument against currency expansion would be to say that the Government is cheating India. It is taking goods in return for bits of paper turned out by its Printing Presses. But such an argument could hardly be advanced in a discussion of financial policy. On such a discussion, a Government's legal right to manufacture a medium of payment is to be taken for granted as also the money value of the medium. Unless anyone would maintain that England was on the verge of bankruptcy, it could not be disputed that the notes issued by the Government of India are covered by a solid asset. The Government of India would not be particularly embarrassed if all the notes in circulation were returned to the Reserve Bank. Because even in that hypothetical extreme case, the Government's credit would be maintained by transferring its assets in

Government securities and discounted commercial paper, the lack of gold, silver and foreign exchange cover and the issue of fresh notes without any relation to the existing currency acts, etc. At the same time public finance is completely disorganised, budgetary deficits go from bad to worse, and the gaps can only be filled by further unlimited issues of paper notes backed only by worthless Government securities. According to generally accepted terms of present day economic literature there is no inflation of currency today in India. Expansion of currency is entirely unavoidable in times of war and in India it is on a most sound basis." (Expansion or Inflation? *Times of India,* March, 5, 1943.)

London to the Indian creditors. Thus, looked at from every point of view, the financial position of the Government of India is quite sound, and it need not be apologetic about its financial policy.[6] But curiously enough, it is. That mystery is the result of the desire of the Government to patronise the brotherhood of big business. Indeed, it is worse. Indian big business, supported by British commercial interests in this country, dictates Government policy. Much too respectful for vested interest, the Government allows its political power to lapse. It will also not fall back on the confidence of the people in order to frustrate a sinister conspiracy against the people.

But what else can the Government do? The purchases must be made and paid for. Is there any other method of payment? On the other hand, Indian businessmen, however patriotic they may be, would not like this roaring business to stop. They want to do business, the more the better. But they are opposed to the Government increasing the medium of payment in the only possible way. But for their profiteering practice, it would not be necessary for the

---

[6] "At the end of three years of war, the most outstanding feature of India's finances is her unimpaired integrity, the impregnable strength, and proven resiliency of the Central and Railway budgets as well as of most Provincial budgets. This country has a unique status in the world in this regard. This uniqueness is particularly noteworthy in three important respects: Firstly, the budgetary deficits in spite of colossal increase in expenditure in defence services, are definitely on the small side; so much so the deficit in the case of India is only a small fraction of the total budget; whereas in most other countries, the deficit is much more than the budget itself. Secondly, there has hardly been any addition to the public debt of India and this stands in pleasant contrast to the experience of countries like Britain and the United States in whose cases the public debt has been piling up at a fast pace. Thirdly, the Government of India which was in a position of debtor to Britain with respect to loans raised in London, is now being transformed into a creditor with millions of pounds to its credit." (*Indian Finance Annual*, 1942. p. 5.)

Government to expand currency even to the present limit.

Therefore, if it is assumed that there is inflation, the most effective check on it would result from a control of profiteering.

In a way, the expansion of currency is uncalled for. Since the war began, the production of primary commodities has not appreciably increased. Industrial production has increased, to some extent. But it is a tiny fraction of the total production of this country. Its expansion adds very little to the total production. Therefore, the same amount of commodities has been exchanged since the war began for a much larger sum of money. To meet the emergency demands of the Government, suppliers have been charging fancy prices. Government must pay. Where is the money? Since the transaction involved a larger amount of money than in circulation before the war, it became necessary to create new money to pay the higher prices charged by war profiteers. That is how currency expansion has taken place. The Government cannot be blamed for it. Profiteers' greed has brought about the situation. So, the way out of the situation is quite obvious.

Some other method of financing the war might have prevented currency expansion. So, let us see how else the Government could pay for war supplies? There are two other methods of financing the war: borrowing and additional taxation. The limit to borrowing is the liquid money already in circulation. But owing to the higher prices charged for supplies it purchases, the Government needs more money than that. So, again it must fall back on its legal right to create new money. The alternative would be to pay the suppliers in bonds or securities. But Indian businessmen are all patriots, wishing the defeat of Britain in this war, and believing in the ability of the Axis Powers to fulfil their wish.

Therefore, they don't want to tie up their fortune in the bonds and securities of the Government whom they want to go. However. since their accepting payment in bonds and securities will prevent currency expansion, the anti-inflationists might persuade them to do so. They do not need the entire payment in cash. Because the primary producers receive only a fraction of what is paid by the Government. The proportion can be judged from the disparity in the expansion of currency and the rise of wholesale prices.

If borrowing takes place through credit operations, ultimately new money will have to be created, so that cash payment may be made by the Government. So, borrowing won't stop "inflation" which is due to war profiteering.

Proceeds of taxation—of the general public—is also limited by the money already in circulation. Unless more money is put into the pocket of the common man, he simply cannot pay additional taxes. Financing the war by taxing property and larger incomes is a sound economic proposition. But assuming that the powerful capitalist and land-owning classes, in a position to pull wires, would be willing to shoulder the burden, the fiduciary position would not improve. They would pay in cheques. The Government must convert its credit into cash. Again, new money will have to be created. The devil of the drama is thus the war profiteer who demands his pound of flesh. The Government had to choose between giving up buying in India or to pay in the only possible manner. The patriots may like the Government to choose the first alternative, unmindful of whatever may happen to the war. But their financial patrons won't be prepared to lose good business.

The only way to check inflation, therefore, will be all-round price control, which again cannot be effective unless the entire stock of commodities is also controlled by the Government.

That solution is, of course, not to the liking of the businessmen. But that is the only way out for the Government, if it wishes to act as the trustee of the Indian people as well as representative of British Democracy. But, unfortunately, it tends to shirk its responsibility as evidenced by its joining the chorus against the bogey of inflation. By doing so, it places itself in a very contradictory position. It pleads guilty to a baseless charge instead of refuting it, which it could easily do. But the pressure of the brotherhood of big business is irresistible.

June 13, 1943.

VI

AN ECONOMIC FALLACY

Apart from the desire to shift the burden of war expenditure on the masses of the people, this talk about inflation is the result of a fallacy of economic thought—a wrong approach to economic problems. It is believed that financial make-shifts or currency manipulations can be the foundation of the economic structure of a country. Indeed, the economic problems of the post-war world are treated in this superficial manner. Some sort of a currency scheme is to be the pivot of an international economic organisation.

Notwithstanding all the clever schemes devised by financial *pandits*, the fact, however, is that production is the essential part of any economic organisation. Trade, credit and finance are agencies of distribution. But commodities must be produced before they are to be distributed. The problems of distribution are secondary problems of economic science. Therefore, it is hardly scientific to ignore the fundamental problem of production while trying to tackle the secondary problems of distribution.

Wealth must be created before it can be distributed. The pulsation of the economic life of a country is determined by the tempo of production. The tempo of production, in its turn, is determined by the means of production. In the light of those guiding principles of economic science it is easy to diagnose the disease from which the economic life of India is suffering. Of course, there are people who do not believe that there is anything wrong with the economic life of this country. They are either ignorant or do not find anything wrong in the economic backwardness of the country, because they derive benefit from it.

No theory can explain the appalling poverty of the Indian masses. Their condition may be slightly better than twenty years or fifty years ago. But the crucial question is: Has India kept pace with the economic progress made by the more advanced countries during the last hundred years? Nobody can answer this question in the affirmative. The next question is: Why has she lagged behind? She is not poor in natural resources, and she has an immense supply of labour which, in the last analysis, creates all new wealth. Apportioning blame and quarreling with contingent factors should not prejudice a scientific investigation. Whatever may have retarded India's economic progress in the past, at present the conditions are all favourable for increasing production, thereby broadening the fundation of her economic life.

The productivity of human labour remains more or less stationary so long as it is primarily and mainly performed on land. Mechanisation of agriculture, which increases the productivity of labour performed therein, is possible only in countries where modern industries are very highly developed. On the other hand, the purchasing power of the home market is the basic condition for an unrestricted expansion of modern industries. It is particularly so when the world market is controlled by older industrial countries.

Having vast natural resources and a plentiful reservoir of labour, India could long ago increase her productivity by equipping labour with modern means of production, and consequently become an economically prosperous country. But the bulk of Indian labour being performed in backward agriculture, the standard of living of the masses remained very low. The home market could not take any increased

8

supply of commodities. That fact placed a limit on production. Modern industries could not expand.

The war has changed the situation. Now the basic obstacle to an unrestricted growth of modern industries can be removed, and India allowed to progress economically. The expansion of currency caused by the emergency of war can be a lever for industrial development of the country. If the new money created for Government purchasing war supplies at higher pices will be so distributed as to reach the pocket of the primary producer, the home market will be able to take more manufactured commodities. Industries will receive an impetus, and once begun, the process will accelerate under its own momentum.

To begin with, industrial production, quickened by greater demand, will absorb more labour which will be withdrawn from land. The total agricultural wages (in the larger sense of remuneration of all labour performed on land) will be distributed to a smaller number of people, each consequently receiving a little more ; the purchasing power of the masses will proportionately increase, and the home market will cease to be static. Increased consumption will augment the impetus to industrial production, which will absorb still more labour, and the cycle will again be soon completed, raising the economic life of the country to a higher level. The process will continue in a geometrical progression. Everybody will be benefited. Industrialists and traders will make greater profit ; improved economic condition of the masses will increase their taxable capacity, reinforcing the foundation of public finance.

Terrified by the bogey of inflation, the Government proposes to check this possibility of general welfare, preferring the economy of scarcity. Instead of welcoming the fortuitous (hypothetical) increase of the purchasing power of the people, it proposes to immobilise it. We have pointed out in previous chapters that the assumption of the peasantry getting benefited by the higher price of agricultural commodities is largely unfounded. Since then, our view has been authoritatively confirmed by the Inflation Officer of the Government of India, according to whom the bulk of the new money created under the pressure of profiteering prices is locked up in banks. That is to say, it belongs to the war suppliers. That also is our view of the situation which constitutes the background of the false cry of inflation. Unless the notes are in circulation, they cannot have any inflationary effect.

In this situation, the wisest policy for the Government would be to mobilise the blocked money either to quicken industrialisation of the country, or for financing the war which has been such a boon for Indian business.[1] As we have pointed out already, this latter alternative will arrest inflationary tendency, if there is any, substituting currency expansion by credit expansion. If the vast amount of new money is left in the possession of its present owners, it is bound to be used in speculative practices, which force up

[1] "At the same time a great deal of capital will be required by private individuals for starting new industries and extending the old ones. This is a large question and can not be dealt with here. I ought to say however that an opportunity is now before us for finding a part of the money required for such purposes. The currency stock of the country has increased from 170 crores before the war to more than 700 crores and may soon be 1000 crores. If all this money is allowed to become active purchasing power as hitherto, prices will soar higher and higher and conditions of life will become intolerable for the common people. But if all that money or as much of it as possible can be effectively impounded by being put into Government loans or some other secure institution, this would give us the funds required for an active development drive after the war when we want it. This is indeed a matter for urgent public concern" (*Nature and Aims of Post-war Reconstruction*: an address delivered to the Rotary Club, Simla by P. J. Thomas.)

prices and thus create the danger of real inflation. If prices are not controlled, and the Government does not want the people to starve and go naked, then more money must be put in their pockets so that they can pay continuously rising prices for the most elementary necessities of life. Then only the dreaded spiral of inflation would begin.

The Government seems to be terrified by that danger of getting caught in the spiral of inflation. The measure recently taken to check the growth of mushroom companies has for its object immobilisation of the money accumulated in the possession of war profiteers. That may be a good intention, but no solution of the problem.[2] As a matter of fact, it is a retrograde measure. Possible industrialisation of the country, thanks to war time business boom, will be prevented, while the policy of complete *laissez faire* as regards trade will permit the use of new money for speculative purposes.

The other contemplated measure against the bogey of inflation is to immobilise the increased purchasing power of the rural population, that is to say, of the peasantry. It will be chasing the will-o'-the-wisp, because the increased purchasing power to be immobilised is very largely a fiction. If it was not a fiction, then it should be mobilised instead

[2] The position with respect to the control of new capital issues was clarified subsequently in a press note issued by the Government of India on July 21, 1943. It makes the position clear by pointing out that "in order to prevent a scamble for the available supplies, which can only result in raising prices still further, it appears best to encourage those industrialists, whose enterprises will directly assist in aiding the war effort or will be in a position to embark upon production of essential consumers' goods at an early date. There is no public purpose in allowing priority to the manufacture of luxury goods, for instance, when the same capital equipment can go to the production of articles in more common use. Without control of capital issues there is no guarantee that such supplies as are available will in fact go to the most suitable applicant."

of being immobilised. But assuming that a very strict and effective control of profiteering will cause the major portion of the new money to reach the peasants, the *per capita* increase of their purchasing power will be hardly a rupee.[3] Thrift is no virtue, has no economic meaning, in the midst of mass poverty or in an atmosphere of want of the most minimum necessities of a bare physical existence. Speaking in the Legislative Assembly during the Budget Debate, Sir Jogendra Singh said: "The purchasing power does not even to-day permit a producer of food to purchase a new set of clothes for himself and his family." The spokesman of the Government of India then proceeded to describe the most minimum needs of the primary producer: "The basic agricultural wage should cover the normal needs of an average worker regarded as a human being in a civilised State. We shall never be satisfied till we feed and clothe our whole population and give them decent dwelling houses to reside in and some share in the gifts which nature distributes."

Evidently, the plan of immobilising purchasing power—granted that it has increased a little—is very premature. There remains still a large lee-way to make. The argument in support of the contemplated plan is that, there being a shortage of manufactured commodities owing to the stoppage of import, their prices will further go up if more liquid money will be left in the possession of the peasantry. Is there no other way than this suicidal economy of scarcity?

[3] "In a vast country like India, there was no need to be alarmed by the currency figures of Rs. 750 crores or even of a thousand crores. In relation to the population of the country and other factors, it was not an intrinsically excessive figure, but it was important to check the tendencies which that figure seemed to indicate." (Sir Jeremy Raisman in the Central Assembly—*Times of India,* August, 13, 1943.)

Indigenous industrial production can be increased to meet the new demand, which can be husbanded by putting more and more money in the pockets of the consuming masses. As a matter of fact, production has been artificially kept down. The plan for the production of cheap standard cloth, for example, has been hanging fire for two years. The whole of the one rupee *per capita* increase in purchasing power granted that it has taken place, will be used up as soon as the promised standard cloth will be placed in the market. For two years, there has been no cloth available for the poor people and to-day they are going half-naked. Nevertheless, there is no guarantee that the much too long delayed agreement between Government and the mill-owners will be implemented by the latter. They have already started manoeuvering for sabotaging it.

Generally speaking, if the purchasing power of the masses has really increased and is likely to increase still more, thanks to the unescapable bogey of inflation, that factor should be allowed to operate as the lever for industrial expansion. Why should the war be a boon only for the profiteers? It can be a blessing also for the people as a whole. Why deprive them of that chance?

A wrong approach to economic problems, determined by a fallacious financial doctrine, is making the Government appear as the devil of the drama. It is accused of obstructing industrial expansion, while in reality Indian moneyed men are themselves reluctant. The suppliers of manufactured or partially manufactured goods ordered by the Government have been relying upon improvised backward methods of production instead of setting up up-to-date factories. Consequently, articles supplied by them are often of inferior quality, falling below the approved standards. The Government must accept them in the absence of any better. The war profiteers function as a closed corporation. There is no competition. Again, the Government is not in such a helpless position.[4] It could control and supervise the entire production of war supplies. In that case, public money would not be wasted in purchasing worthless goods, and thanks to a guaranteed market, a broad foundation of modern industry would be laid.

The capitalists do not want that, although they accuse the Government for obstructing industrial expansion, and the Government obligingly makes it easy for them to do so. They are afraid of the hypothetical post-war slump. It is taken for granted that, as soon as the war is over, prices will fall and the slightly increased purchasing power of the masses will again vanish. Industrial plants set up for manufacturing war supplies will after the war have to produce consumers' goods, which must be sold at reasonable prices to find any market. That is not an attractive perspective for businessmen used to profiteering. Therefore, they are reluctant to build up-to-date industrial plants during the war, and lock up their money in capital goods which, according to profiteers' calculation, will not be a good enough investment. Moreover, by restricting production during the war, they will make the largest possible profit, while the opportunity to do so lasts, so that they will be able after the war to scrap improvised establishment in which very little money has been invested.

The Government also share the fear of post-war slump, which is not unavoidable. Evidently, the pressure of the

---

[4] "But what is required in order to achieve industrial development today and after the war is a more direct and active association of the Government with the industrial activity. If private enterprise will not come forward to establish the key, basic and defence industries the Government must itself arrange for their establishment." (*Industrialisation* by P. S. Lokanathan. p. 17.)

brotherhood of big business is in operation. If the profit motive was not granted sovereignty over the economic life of the country, the Government could take things in hand and lay both the bogeys,—of inflation and post-war slump.

Very concrete recommendations in this respect were made by the Grady Mission. The report was quietly shelved by the Government because Big Business did not like it. A representative of the brotherhood of big business occupied a high position in the Government of India at that time. He simply forced the hands of the Government by publicly disparaging the recommendations of the report. It is clear from the Report that Big Business did not favour expansion of production: "Some believe that maximum production has been reached under a voluntary system actuated by the profit motive."

The Grady Mission, which represented the interests of the United Nations, evidently did not accept the view of Indian Big Business. It expressed the view that "much remains to be done before a complete mobilisation of India's resources is attained." Then, referring to the practice in Britain and the United States, the Mission made the following very specific recommendation:

"The twofold problem of augmenting the production of certain peace-time commodities required for war, and of converting peace-time industries to new war production, can be solved only by strong centralised power vested in, and exercised by, Government. . . A basic change in production technique is needed; and mass production methods must be introduced. This will be a difficult task, involving the provision of new equipment, the transfer of equipment from one shop to another, and the re-arrangement of equipment within existing shops. But the task must be undertaken, and with it the more rigid control of materials, priorities and prices."

The recommendations put the Government in a fix. Would it dare make general interest, including the cause of the United Nations, prevail over the selfishness of the brotherhood of big business? Had not the tide of military events turned before long, the overriding demand for war supplies might have compelled the Government to break down the wilful resistance of big business, and place India on the road of the much delayed economic progress. There would be no difficulty about machine tools which are indispensable for modern industrial plants. The Grady Mission guaranteed their supply from the United States.

The Mission came to investigate the possibilities of India becoming the arsenal of the East. It found her fully equipped to rise up to the occasion. Soon afterwards, while the Government of India was still hesitating in the face of the resistance of the brotherhood of big business, the tide of war turned. The danger of invasion from the West having receded, the urgency of building up in India a fully equipped modern supply base disappeared. The Government of India heaved a sigh of relief and gave in to big business without any qualm of conscience.

But the war is not yet over. The problem of supplying China has not yet been solved. Industrialisation of India can solve that problem. Then, major battles will have to be fought to drive the Japs out of Burma and other countries they have occupied. So, the necessity of India becoming a well-equipped modern supply base still remains. With the opening of the Mediterranean route, the chances of fulfilling that necessity will increase. Finally, and above all other considerations, there is the necessity of India's own economic progress, which will be a condition for her post-war reconstruction and her contribution to the reconstruction of the world. All these immediate and remote considerations are being seriously prejudiced by the fallacious economic doctrine which is dictating the financial policy of the Government of India.

June 20, 1943.

VII

THE SPECTRE OF POST-WAR SLUMP

As long as the war lasts, the bogey of inflation cannot be laid ; and it being only a bogey, need not frighten people who are not obsessed with fallacious economic doctrines.

War supplies must be purchased, and the Government, having preferred the policy of paying in cash, must create new money. The only possible check on currency expansion, in the given situation, is rigid control of profiteering which is also a guarantee that the benefit of higher prices goes to the producers. In that case, new money will be very widely distributed, and the war time currency expansion will have to go very far before it can have any inflationary effect.

Money is a medium of exchange. The economic life of a country is not essentially affected one way or the other by a larger or smaller amount of money being in circulation. As a matter of fact, cheap money gives an incentive to production, whereas hard money is advantageous for financiers who are engaged in the entirely useless and parasitic occupation of trading with the medium of exchange. Therefore, in so far as the war currency expansion creates new money, and assuming that it will find its way to the mass of primary producers, there is nothing to be alarmed in the present situation.

But a considerable part of the new money is not in circulation. It is the share of profiteering traders who are making money by charging higher prices for war supplies. That money is either being used for speculative financial transactions, or is lying locked up in banks. In addition to being a source of economic evil, inasmuch as it promotes profiteering, the larger portion of the newly created money is a frozen asset. It can be made to flow in the economic veins of the country in two ways: Through the control of profiteering it can be so directed as to reach the masses of primary producers, and thus become a medium of exchange; or, it can be transformed into capital, that is to say, means of production. Indeed, the economic life of the country will be invigorated by making the new money serve the double purposes of a medium of exchange and means of production.

The function of the economic organisation of any country is to produce and supply the needs of the people. Production is the basic factor. Commodities must be produced before they can be exchanged. The amount of money in circulation increases in proportion to the volume of commodities to be exchanged; or, when higher prices are charged, for the same amount of commodities. The present financial position of the Government has been brought about by this latter cause, which will remain in operation, at least partially, so long as the war lasts. Higher prices of primary commodities, particularly in an agricultural country like India, are not an evil, provided that the additional money put in circulation thereby finds its way to the producer. More medium of exchange in the hands of the needy consuming masses will quicken the process of exchange. The problem, then, will be how to supply the increased demand. Greater demand can be satisfied only by increased production. So, in the last analysis, it is the problem of production which confronts the economic organisation of the country to-day. No useful purpose will be served by shirking the problem on the pretext of inflation.

Can the productive capacity of the country be increased under the handicap of the war emergency? Is it an economic necessity to do so? The answer to this latter question is given by an analysis of the economic condition of the masses of the people. Are their most elementary requirements adequately satisfied? Let the answer to this fundamental question be given in the words of a spokesman of the Government.

During the last budget debate, the representative of British business interests in this country drew the attention of the Government to "the dangers inherent in increased purchasing power due to the so-called inflation." Incidentally, he suggested the correct remedy for the apparent disease, because he also enquired what was the Government doing for introducing effective price control. At that time, the Finance Member had not yet come under the spell of the bogey. On the contrary, he welcomed the increased purchasing power as an economic blessing, because "an increase in prices of agricultural produce meant reduction in the burden of agricultural debt." The crux of the situation, however, was laid bare by the member in charge of Education, Health and Land, participating in the debate. He said:

"Even in normal years our production is not sufficient to give all the people a balanced diet and the purchasing power which frightens Sir Henry Richardson does not even to-day permit a producer of food to purchase a new set of clothes for himself and his family. We may hope that the volume of money in circulation will stimulate economic progress in this land of low purchasing power. The basic agricultural wage should cover the normal needs of an average worker regarded, as a human being in a civilised State. I am sure Sir Henry Richardson will never be satisfied till we feed and clothe our whole population and give them decent dwelling houses to reside in, and some share in the gifts of nature."

Evidently, the bulk of the population is not adequately supplied. Therefore, it is legitimate to say that the economic organisation of the country is not performing its function. Until recently, the demand was dormant. People needed things essential for bare physical existence, but did not have the money to buy them. Now the demand has become active to the extent that a part of the new money created for purchasing was supplies has filtered down to the primary producer. Consequently, more commodities will not depress the market. Traders should not complain against the so-called inflation, and the productive capacity of the country can be given a free play without in any way upsetting the economic organisation.

The demand being mostly for manufactured articles, what is needed is industrial expansion. All the three conditions for unrestricted industrialisation of the country are mature. There is plenty of labour ; raw materials are abundant ; and at last there is an internal market which can be progressively enlarged by quickening the economic life of the country. The idle money in the possession of war profiteers can be immediately converted into productive capital. Rapid development of industries will not only strengthen India's position as a base for war supplies, but will also harness the slightly increased purchasing power to rationalise the unbalanced economic life of the country. Consequently, currency expansion or cheapening money will cease to give rise to the bogey of inflation.

The proposed immobilisation of the hypothetically increased purchasing power can be justified only on the assumption that the commodities in demand must be imported ; that they cannot be manufactured in the country.

If that was really true, then people, must go short so long as the war will interfere with imports. In that case, it would be a bad financial policy on the part of the Government to leave surplus money in the possession of the people, as that would certainly force prices up. That is the case, for instance, with certain articles of food in Britain. They cannot be grown in the country. In import, the priority of shipping and necessary protection must be conceded to raw materials for war industries. But the situation in this country is not analogous.

Here, the shortage is of manufactured goods. The price of food stuff and other primary commodities has gone up not due to any shortage, but because of an artificially created scarcity. Manufactured articles for the daily use of the common people in this country used to be very largely imported before the war. War conditions have stopped that import. But is it necessary for the people to do without them? Can they not be manufactured in the country? Will the manufacture of consumers' goods interfere with war production? These are the questions to be carefully examined and honestly answered by those who control the economic life of the country.

All manufactured articles needed for daily consumption can be produced in the country. As a matter of fact, for a fairly long time they have been produced in the country in ever increasing quantities. The shortage thus being not absolute, the people need not be compelled to go without them.

The demand being there, the question is if labour and raw materials can be spared from war production. It is obvious that Indian resources on either account are almost unlimited. Moreover, it has been admitted that even for war production they are not being fully utilised. The recommendations of the Grady Mission in this respect have not been acted upon, because private industrialists are of the opinion that "maximum production has been reached under a voluntary system actuated by profit motive". (*Grady Mission Report*). The Mission, however, was emphatically of the opinion that India's war production had reached nowhere near the maximum, and that "much remains to be done before a complete mobilisation of India's resources is attained."

However near the end of the war in Europe may appear to be, it would be foolish to be optimistic about perspective in the East. Thus, the necessity of transforming India into the arsenal of the East still remains. In any case, she must be the base of supply for a protracted war. And the supplies for modern warfare are very largely industrial. Therefore, the task of rationalising and expanding India's war production still remains to be accomplished. And it cannot be done except as recommended by the Grady Mission. The substance of the recommendations was Government control and some restriction of the profit motive. If the reluctance to act according to those recommendations could not be overcome under the pressure of war emergency, there is little chance of industrial expansion for the supply of consumers' goods. For in this respect also, a certain measure of Government control and some limitation of unrestricted profit motive are indispensable.

As regards other factors, there cannot be any doubt about the necessary supply of labour for the production of consumers' goods. As a matter of fact, even to-day, when a small fraction of India's total reservior of labour has been absorbed in war production, a vast amount of it is still wasted on land. That waste of the basic asset of national economy is the primary cause of India's economic backwardness. Withdrawal of labour from land for industrial employment will not decrease foood production in the least. The total amount of food produced in this country is not relatively very large. It is hardly enough to feed the people. It can be produced with a fraction of the labour now being wasted on land. Some relief of the pressure on land will stabilise the basic industry of agriculture. If that process goes far enough, it will cure the evil of sub-infeudation of land and ultimately help the solution of the basic problem of Indian economy, namely, the agrarian problem. Therefore, supply of labour presents absolutely no difficuulty as regards industrialisation.

Regarding the supply of raw materials, the position is also safe, although somewhat complicated. Manufactured articles required by the Indian masses will be so elementary still for some time, that raw materials needed for the purpose will not mean interference with war production.

Finally, there is the question of capital goods for building up modern industrial plants. That does present some difficulty created by the war conditions. But with the opening of the Mediterranean route, some amelioration in that respect can be expected. The Grady Mission promised supply of American machinery which would be required for the expansion and rationalisation of war production recommended by it. That promise can be implemented now more easily than before. The sterling balances accumulating in London can be used for this purpose. So, from all points of view, industrialisation of the country is now quite practicable as well as necessary.

Why, then, is it not done? In addition to the bogey of inflation, the Government as well as big business is terrified by the spectre of post-war slump.[1] The economy of scarcity advocated on the ground of imaginary inflation is expected to create a guarantee against the spectre of post-war slump. That is a very short-sighted policy which would sacrifice general welfare, not only of this country, but of the world as a whole, for the immediate selfish interest of the business community. Assuming honesty in this short-sightedness, it is to be ascribed to the fallacious economic doctrine which puts the economic organisation of a country on its head. Those who are terrified by the spectre of post-war reconstruction should know that it can be exorcised, under the given situation, only by the bogey of inflation which frightens them so much. If expansion of currency increases the purchasing power of the people, there will be no post-war slump. By the time industries built during the war will have to be shifted to the production of consumers' goods,

---

[1] The fear of the post-war slump has been most typically expressed in the following passage which occurs in a publication of Prof. K. T. Shah, "The purchases on the British account have, moreover, their own reaction upon the industrial position of the country. Several industries, in fact, have been established anew, and existing ones expanded and reconditioned, to meet these demands. But the industries thus set up under the impetus of the war, must face a different prospect when once the war comes to an end; and the surplus stores and materials left over after the war are dumped upon the market. Demand would then be reoriented into the normal peacetime channels; and will not provide the present inflated prices which keep these industries flourishing today. It is doubtful if those who now own and manage these industries make adequate provision from their present huge profits, to safeguard and maintain their position when the war-born flush is finished. It is possible also that they may take longer in this country to readjust themselves to peacetime requirements than in other countries. In the meanwhile, there may supervene a depression of much greater severity and duration than is commonly realised." (*How India Pays For The War*, page 44.) Similar fear has been expressed by almost all those who have pleaded for the need of combating what they have styled as the inflationary situation in the country.

the old restricting factor of a limited home market will disappear. Consequently, there will be no slump.

The problem is difficult of immediate solution: it is how to put in the market a sufficient quantity of manufactured goods for daily consumption, so that there may not be idle money about to force up prices. To solve that problem by the easy method of immobilising purchasing power, is evidently suicidal. That approach to the problem creates the terrifying spectre of post-war slump. Because the very idea of immobilising purchasing power assumes that it has reached the limit and should not be allowed to grow further. The result of this policy will be to prevent the creation of active demand, which alone will protect the economic organisation of the country against the danger of a post-war slump.

The suicidal immediate solution of the problem is dictated by the desire to arrest a continuous rise of prices which, it is apprehended, will produce the dreaded spiral of inflation. The desire is very laudable. But it could be attained more successfully through other means. Cloth is the article of consumption required by the masses next in importance only to food. For two years, the supply has been totally inadequate. It is an indisputable fact that the textile industry can produce enough cloth to supply the demand which may have increased slightly thanks to a little more money in the hand of the masses. A whole variety of industries to produce elementary articles of daily necessity can be built up with machines and tools manufactured in the country. Then, if war industries expand, it will be possible to reserve a certain part of their productive capacity for the manufacture of consumers' goods.

Briefly speaking, the policy should be not to discourage the slight expansion of the internal market caused by war conditions. Instead, it should be husbanded and industries should be allowed to grow, in order not only to supply the demand, but to stimulate it with greater supplies. The expansion of currency has created conditions for this policy. There is money to be used as medium of exchange, and also to be converted into capital. If that is done, there will be no necessity to prefer the economy of scarcity under the imaginary threat of post-war slump. If there will be a post-war slump, the present financial policy of the Government and the greed of big business, which is dictating this policy, will be responsible.

June 27, 1943.

VIII

PLANNED ECONOMY—I

THE exigencies of war production have revolutionised the economic organisation of Great Britain. Private ownership of the means of production has indeed not yet been formally and legally abolished. But State control has gone far enough to produce that effect virtually. The rationalisation and regimentation of industry, introduced for speeding up the production of war supplies, include such measures as "absolute prohibition of the manfacture of certain goods, the taking over by or for the Government of plants that are not being efficiently worked and instructions to industry to manufacture specified goods, whatever dislocation or loss of profit any such moves may cost."

In its report, the American Technical Mission, which visited India in summer 1942, cited the above evidence of the State control of industries in Great Britain and United States, in support of its recommendation for similar measures to be taken by the Government of India. The Mission further observed that "under the emergency of war, there must be unification, co-ordination, restriction of initiative, subordination of the profit incentive and complete concentration of the nation through its Government." It testified that the War had brought about a similar revolutionary reorganisation of the industrial life of Great Britain.

Will the process be reversed after the war? The answer to this question necessarily enters into any scheme of post-war reconstruction. A large measure of Government control of the economic life of the nation was introduced in Great Britain also during the last world war. But after the war, all control was removed. It is apprehended that the same thing may happen this time also. But the chaotic consequences of the restoration of *laissez faire* after the last war have their lessons, which are not likely to be disregarded this time. Those consequences threw the economic organisation of the entire world out of balance during the period between the two wars, and contributed to the rise of Fascism. In other words, they were the cause of the present war. Therefore, a growing number of businessmen and economic thinkers are anxious to see that the mistake is not repeated.

The British Labour Party, which will most probably have a greater share in the Government after the war, discussed this question at length in its recent annual conference. The opinion was emphatically registered that the restriction on competitive private enterprise imposed during the war should continue afterwards. The parliamentary leader of the Labour Party, who is also the Deputy Prime Minister, concluded the debate with the significant declaration that the party would insist upon continuation of the revolutionary re-organisation of the economic life of the country even after the war. This clear voice of labour is bound to influence the scheme of post-war reconstruction of Britain.

There are other indications to the effect that the revolutionary changes introduced under the pressure of the war emergency have come to stay. A special committee of the London Chamber of Commerce, in its report submitted in May, 1942, outlined "the general principles of a post-war economy." The following passage occurs in that report: "It is widely admitted that there was something radically wrong with our economic system. There has not, however, been the same readiness to recognise that there must be serious error in our economic thinking in order to produce absurd results."

That is a bold admission of the necessity for a radical re-adjustment of economic relations. The war time control of the process of production and distribution represents an advance in that direction. Therefore, far-sighted business-men also are veering round to the opinion that the changes brought about during the war have come to stay.

What was "radically wrong with our economic system?" It was disregard for the original purpose of production. Instead of producing goods for the use of the community, industries produced only for exchange. In other words, production was not planned. It was chaotic. The result of such an economic system inevitably was recurring depression and dislocation of the economic life caused by so-called over-production. Ultimately, the result culminated in "the wretched financial history of the twenty-one years between the two wars", against the repetition of which the report of the special committee of the London Chamber of Commerce sounds a warning, and recommends preventive measures.

The report lays the finger on the sore spot of the radically wrong economic system by coming to the conclusion that "maximum production was achieved by a complex system of cut-throat competition for cheapness." Then it proceeds to make the following important statement: "Nations now recognise that the maintenance of a correct balance between industry and agriculture is essential both for social stability and for the health and happiness of the community."

Evidently, this result cannot be obtained, unless production and distribution take place according to co-ordinated plan in pursuance of a common purpose. It is equally evident that such a re-organisation of the economic life of a country is not possible without a central direction and a minimum measure of State control. Industries built with the collective asset of the nation must produce what is necessary for promoting the welfare of the nation. Industry cannot perform its function, if it is allowed to be guided by the profit motive of individual businessmen engaged in cut-throat competition. In the time of war, supplies for the armed forces is the predominating need of the nation. The Government finds it necessary, and considers it to be within its legal competence, to see that industries produce what the nation needs. Why should not the same principle be in operation in peace time also? The failure to build upon the experience gained during the last world war led to the "wretched history of the twenty-one years between the two wars." Therefore, this time the lesson of history is sure to be learned, because otherwise the wretched history will repeat itself in a more aggravated form, and on a much larger scale.

A boldly written document called "A Twentieth Century Economic System" which is incorporated in the Report of the Special Committee of the London Chamber of Commerce, anticipated the resolution of the British Labour Party Conference. It declared: "One of the crying needs of our civilization is the measure of material security and stability, and this system can provide neither. It ignores human nature and will not be tolerated by the workers in the second half of the nineteenth century."

That unanimity of the opinion of labour and of at least the more enlightened section of businessmen guarantees that the war time reorganisation of the economic life of Britain will continue after the war as the basis of post-war reconstruction.

The Report of the Special Committee of the Association of British Chambers of Commerce on "Post-War Indusrial Reconstruction" is even more explicit. It says: "Each industry should be responsible for the planning of its own policy and, to ensure that the policy of each industry fits into the post-war scheme of reconstruction as a whole, it should be agreed by a council consisting of representatives of industry, commerce and labour, to be approved by the Board of Trade, and to be known as the Council of Industry. The work of this Council would ensure co-operation between His Majesty's Government and private enterprise, in order that trade and industry might be carried on for the benefit of the community as a whole."

It may be difficult to say now how things will exactly shape after the war. But the tendency is clear enough to permit the conclusion that the mistake committed after the last great war will not be repeated in Britain. The need of planning industrial production has been realised, and the experience of the war has taught that it can be planned without any injury to the process of production and distribution.

Will India be similarly benefited by the economic consequences of the war? If she had participated in it voluntarily and wholeheartedly, the question would not have arisen. Because in that case, her economic life also would have undergone a revolutionary reorganisation. The American Technical Mission recommended "a basic change in production technique and mass production". It pointed out the far-reaching implications of the recommendation "involving the provision of new equipment, the transfer of equipment from one shop to another, and the rearrangement of equipment within existing shops . . . and more rigid control of materials, priorities and prices." The Government of India formally accepted the recommendations, but failed to act up to them.

In releasing a summary of the Report to the press the then Supply Member of the Government of India observed:

"The Mission recommends a much more drastic rationalisation and regimentation of industry than has hitherto been attempted in India. There are obvious difficulties about wholesale rationalisation and regimentation." This observation reflected the opinion of the Indian business community rather than of the Government of India. Because this view of the situation prevented a sufficient expansion of production which would have seriously endangered the defence of the country, had not the tide of the war turned. That fortunate eventuality persuaded the Government to be guided by the selfish view of the business community, and thus deprive India of the benefit of a rationalisation and reorganisation of her economic life under the pressure of the war emergency. That being the case, there is grave doubt regarding the post-war economic reconstruction of India. The guarantee against India remaining saddled with a radically wrong economic system even when Britain will outgrow it, however, is provided by the necessity that the world as a whole must be rationalised and reorganised economically if it is to avoid a repetition of the wretched history of the period between the two wars.

The basis for a new economic system has been laid by the war. Experience has proved that production can be planned, and that planned production eliminates the chaos of distribution. But the experience of war economy has also proved that production cannot be planned without placing some restriction on private ownership. In the absence of any systematic and effective control by the Government, both production and distribution in India have remained in a chaotic state. Even the distribution of food to the people could not be planned, because the Government was reluctant to interfere with the freedom of trade. If these chaotic practices will continue after the war, the imaginary post-war slump will be a rude reality, and endless hardships and incalculable suffering will be the share of the masses of the population. Industrial stagnation and the consequent general economic disorganisation of India will place serious obstacles to a rational post-war reconstruction of the world. Is it, then, not possible to plan Indian economy, notwithstanding the chaotic conditions which are allowed to prevail during the war? It is possible, because in the last analysis the war has laid down the foundation for planned economy also for India. The only obstacle is the unlimited right of private ownership and the reluctance to abandon an economic system which has proved to be radically wrong because it is antiquated. If the Government of India would only be guided by the sound principles enunciated in the Report of the London Chamber of Commerce, planned economy could be introduced in India, and her economic life invigorated consequently.

India will emerge out of this war a creditor nation. In the form of piling up sterling balances in London, she has already a very considerable international credit. What to do with this credit? There is a good deal of disagreement on this question. Immediately, it has permitted an expansion of currency, which is required for making war purchases. The sterling balances transferred to the Issue Department of the Reserve Bank can be the covering for many times more expanded currency. If production was not artificially restricted owing to the fear of an imaginary post-war slump, the currency expansion with an adequate covering would increase the purchasing power of the people, thus giving a tremendous impetus to the economic life of the country. The deliberately practised economy of scarcity results in an inflationary tendency even in the present state of currency expansion. The bogey of inflation, in its turn, scares the Government, and it is considering the suicidal policy of checking the possibility of a slight increase of purchasing power created by the conditions of war.

The sterling balances, however, can be used in an entirely different manner, quickening the industrial life of India. Immediately, it can be the lever for increasing the purchasing power of the people by providing the covering for a furher expansion of currency. That would not be inflation, if side by side industrial production is allowed to expand. It has already been pointed out that there is no insuperable obstacle to increasing the production of consumers' goods to cope with the increased purchasing power. This immediate policy will create conditions for a long term policy of post-war reconstruction on the sound financial basis of India's credit abroad.

Already last year, the Government decided to create a reconstruction fund out of the sterling balances. In his budget speech this year, the Finance Member declared that he would abandon the scheme if the Opposition so desired. That was a concession to Indian businessmen who still remain wedded to the radically wrong system of the economy of scarcity. There is no reason for the Government to make that concession, because the sterling balances are nobody's private property. They belong to the public exchequer, and therefore it is within the legal competence of the Government to use it for promoting public welfare. That may be done by using the credit for purchasing capital goods necessary for a rapid industrialisation of the country.

After the war, it may not be possible to use India's sterling balances in London for any other purpose. The general principles of post-war economy formulated in the Report of the London Chamber include the suggestion that international payments in future should be received only in goods and services. That is a very sound principle, which will undermine the practice of more prosperous and powerful nations getting others into "unpayable indebtedness". That practice is the foundation of modern Imperialism.

The Indian businessmen's outcry against inflation is most probably the result of the desire that the Government of India should pay for its war purchases by transferring the sterling balances to the credit of private businessmen instead of cash payment. If the Indian Government would oblige the ambitious businessmen, then the latter would have their capital invested abroad, where great industrial activities due to post-war reconstruction would make capital investment more profitable. While still clamouring for a National Government, Indian businessmen are developing imperialist ambitions. Only they are too late in appearing on the scene, because Imperialism is a part of the radically wrong economic system which has been irreparably undermined by this war.

But they are day-dreaming. Whatever may be their heart's desire, they will have to adjust themselves to the post-war world economy. A fundamental principle of that economy will be to keep international credit blocked until it is used for buying goods or services. So, ultimately, India's credit balances in London, whether they will remain part of the public exchequer or be transferred by an obliging Government to the credit of private businessmen, will have to be used for purchasing goods. The first question is what sort of goods they will be. Assuming that only consumers' goods will be bought, the purchasing power of the Indian masses will have to be increased so that the goods imported could be consumed. Therefore, the London Chamber of Commerce has very rightly come to the conclusion that the crux of the problem of post-war reconstruction will be how to raise the purchasing power of the people in all the countries. It cannot be done in India except on the basis of a planned economy, and planned economy is not possible unless the rights of private ownership are restricted

The war might be won without the Government of India taking any measure with that revolutionary implication But measures of that nature will be indispensable for India's post-war economic reconstruction. Neither the bogey of inflation nor the spectre of post-war slump should scare far-sighted statesmen away from that reality of the situation, which they will have to face.

July 11, 1943.

IX

PLANNED ECONOMY—II

Private ownership of the means of production has been a decisive check on the expansion of the production of war supplies. India, and perhaps the United Nations, escaped the disastrous consequences thereof only thanks to the miracle performed by the Red Army, and the Red Army could perform the miracle because it was supplied by an industrial system built on the basis of planned economy.

Last summer it was a matter of touch and go. Had the Fascist hordes succeeded in breaking through the Caucasus, as they very nearly did, the defence of India would be a hopeless proposition. She would most probably be overrun by the invader, not thanks to his valour, but due to her own economic weakness and also to the failure of the Government to remove that weakness because of an excessive respect for private ownership. The privileged position of those controlling (throttling would be the more appropriate term) the economic life of the country was not to be touched, even when they were not only making a racket of the profitable business of war supplies, but were actually engaged in a criminal conspiracy to sabotage the defence of the country.

Fortunately, the tide of war turned, and India was spared the disaster. The rulers relapsed into complacency, and would not learn from the lesson. They might have taken courage in both hands, and liberated war production from the shackles of private ownership and profit motive, had India come nearer to the disaster. It did not come to that ; consequently India's economic life was deprived of the benefit of revolutionary changes under the impact of war emergency. Her productive capacity remained restricted by private ownership of the means of production.

Pursuing the short-sighted policy of least resistance, the Government did not act even according to the recommendations of the American Technical Mission, which were opposed by big business haunted by the nightmare of post-war slump. The adverse consequences of that short-sighted policy may still have to be experienced. One of the major operations of this war for the recovery of Burma, without which Japan cannot be driven out of China and finally defeated, will have to be based on India. Indeed, India will have to be the source of supply also for the battles to drive the Japs out of Malasia. No industrially backward country can be a dependable base for modern armies. So, expansion of India's industrial production still remains a condition for the final victory of the United Nations. Experience has proved that the condition can not be fulfilled within the limits of unrestricted private ownership.

Even in countries where war efforts are not sabotaged for selfish political motives, privileges of private ownership had to be severely curtailed to guarantee maximum production of war supplies. To meet the emergencies of war, production had to be planned, and no planning was possible without subordinating private initiative, that is, competitive production, to State control. The war thus has been instrumental in shifting production back to the basis of its original purpose. Under the impact of the emergency of war, industries have been compelled to produce for the use of the community, and not exclusively with the purpose of obtaining the highest possible profit for the owners of the means of production. Only under that compulsion, exercised by the Government in behalf of the community as a whole, could maximum production be guaranteed. Since the compulsion represented the weal of society, it was no compulsion. It was elimination of the unsocial, if not actually anti-social, factors in the economic life of the country.

In India, the Government did not do what was done in other countries to guarantee maximum production of war supplies, although in this country the apparent compulsion was more necessary, the Indian industrialists, in addition to the selfishness of their class, having not their heart in the camp of the United Nations. While production and more production was the crying need of the moment, there was industrial sabotage instead of increased production. Still the Government would not learn. It is difficult to understand why the British rulers of this country should have greater respect for private ownership than the Government in Britain. It is a veritable case of being more royalist than the King.

If private ownership of the means of production has prevented the urgently needed expansion of war production and actually sabotaged production of consumers' goods, private control of the channels of distribution has created an artificial scarcity of primary necessities. Consequently, not only are the masses of consumers subjected to great hardship, but the political atmosphere of the country has become dangerously inflammable. It is a matter of experience that Government's plan to guarantee supply of food and other primary necessities to the civil population has repeatedly miscarried because of the reluctance to restrict the freedom of prviate trade. Freedom of trade has degenerated into licence for hoarding and profiteering, which anti-social practices cannot be checked unless the supply and distribution of primary necessities are controlled by the Government as in Britain.[1]

From this brief review of the situation, it follows that planning guarantees greater production and equitable distribution, and that planned economy is not consistent with unrestricted private ownership. This lesson, already learned by wise politicians and far-sighted businessmen, promises to be one of the positive outcomes of this war. It is now generally agreed that post-war reconstruction must be planned. But the implication of planning an economy is not yet fully grasped, although the rich experience of war time practice is there to be learned from.

---

[1] "Control measures succeed in proportion as they are thorough and comprehensive and half measures are often worse than no measures. And then their actual success turns greatly upon people's belief in their effectiveness If anything happens to shake that faith, or if the Government fails to create it, then all the forces that normally work against control gather strength and make its final breakdown a mere matter of time This is what has happened in our country For quite some time after the war had broken out, the Government watched the situation anxiously or otherwise.—But there was no indication of a comprehensive plan, either it was not there or it was the precious secret of a few brains. The problem deepened and widened, there were temporary phases of flat movements of prices or even transient depressions. But these were deceptive and only helped to postpone a general attack. The Government took piecemeal measures here and there, leaving vast areas to hoarders and profiteers, and even in the narrow sectors that it chose for attack, it was not sufficiently vigorous and farsighted to anticipate and provide against dangerous but extremely probable contingencies. Black markets developed extensively and turned the official control into a costly joke for the law-abiding citizen. The anti-climax came with the announcement of de-control in respect of important foodstuffs. We now hope to achieve by decontrol those aims of reasonable prices and equitable distribution which control was once supposed to encompass. We live to learn. The decontrol might or might not solve the problem of engineered shortages and surreptitious profiteering, I have great doubts if it will. But it certainly takes out of the armoury of public finance an important weapon to fight inflation." (*War and the Rupee* by D. Ghosh, page 27-28.)

The error of economic thinking was to consider private ownership indispensable even when it only produced "absurd results." That error precipitated the recurring crises of over-production even when "a large percentage of population (in prosperous countries) remained underfed, ill-clothed and ill-housed." Production on the basis of private ownership takes place for exchange. Goods are produced not for supplying the needy, but to be exchanged profitably. And, as the London Chamber of Commerce Report says, "goods are not for long produced if there are no buyers." The Report, therefore, comes to the conclusion that "there can be no such thing as general over-production. The real trouble is under-consumption."

The absurdities of a radically wrong economic system, can be removed by planning production, by producing to supply human demand, instead of equating supply with effective demand. No planning can be successful unless it is guided by the principle that the purpose of production is to meet the requirements of mankind. Once that principle is accepted, there can never be over-production, and the spectre of post-war slump will disappear. The laying of that ghost may still let India have the benefit of war time planning of production and distribution, which in its turn will lay down the foundation of her post-war reconstruction.

Unless the consumption of manufactured goods is stimulated, India's economic life will be seriously disorganised after the war. She will be confronted with the problem of using up her international credit built up during the war. Payment will have to be received in goods. Large imports of manufactured goods will intensify competition with home industries. Prices will fall, and wages will be attacked to reduce the cost of production. For the same reason, prices of raw materials will also go down. There will be an all-round sinking of purchasing power, just when the market will be flooded with goods. Evidently, the catastrophe can be avoided only by increasing the purchasing power of the masses. As a matter of fact, the central problem of the post-war reconstruction of the world will be "how to distribute purchasing power to the masses of the people?" (*Report of the London Chamber of Commerce*).

If, to protect Indian industries against competition, India will not take payment in consumers' goods, the alternative will be to import capital goods. But new industries will before long add to the production of consumers' goods inside the country. India will experience the absurdity of over-production, even when the bulk of her population will remain deprived of most elementary human amenities.

Evidently, increased purchasing power of the masses alone can guarantee Indian economy against the post-war slump. How to create that guarantee? How to plan Indian economy? That is the problem. Private ownership of the means of production and private control of the channels of distribution render the problem baffling. But the problem must be solved if India herself is to progress economically, and is not to be an obstacle to the post-war reconstruction of the world. The war has created conditions for a solution of the problem. It has enabled India to pile up sterling balances in London which can serve as a powerful lever for her economic progress. On the basis of her international credit, *treated as a national asset,* her economic life can be planned.

India's economic life has been caught in a vicious circle, so to say. Increased productivity of labour is the primary condition for the economic progress of any country. India possesses an almost inexhaustible supply of labour. Nevertheless, she has remained economically stagnant because the productivity of her labour could not be progressively increased. Unless modern industries grow, labour cannot be withdrawn from land ; but on the other hand, industrial development is conditional upon a rising purchasing power of the masses. While agriculture still remains the basic industry of the country, retarding the growth of modern industries by keeping the bulk of labour tied to the land, increase of the purchasing power of the masses is conditional upon a radical change in the relation of property in land. The vicious circle of Indian economy was the result of opposition to those changes necessary for the welfare of the community as a whole.

The vicious circle can now be broken in a different manner. The sterling balances can serve the purpose. As a matter of fact, they are already operating in that sense. But there is a desire on the part of Indian vested interests, patronised by the Government, to arrest that operation. The desire is expressed in the outcry against the so-called inflation and in the suicidal plan of immobilising purchasing power. What should be done, however, is to expand currency still more on the basis of sterling securities. But that alone will not serve the purpose, unless rigorous measures are taken so that the benefit of higher prices goes to the primary producers, increasing their purchasing power. More money in the hand of the peasantry, in an agricultural country like India, will be a tremendous impetus to the economic life of the country. Human demand will be converted into effective demand. The resulting expansion of market will enable India to use a considerable part of her international credit by importing consumers' goods. Thanks to the expansion of the market, import will not adversely affect home production. Increased purchasing power of the masses, indeed, will create conditions favourable for the development of home industries. That again will enable India to receive payments in capital goods. Growth of modern industries, in its turn, will withdraw labour from land, and consequently the total productivity of Indian labour will increase. The relief of the pressure on land, again, will make rationalisation of agriculture possible. Rationalisation will increase the productivity of agriculture, increasing the purchasing power of the peasantry still further.

The bogey of inflation stands on the way towards this economic prosperity and all-round progress. The bogey is raised by vested interest. The Government seems to be anxious to earmark the bulk of the sterling balances for the purchase of capital goods after the war. It is believed that will be helpful for British industries. If the capital goods will be used for the industrial reconstruction of the country, the problem of increasing the purchasing power of the Indian masses must be tackled from now on. Otherwise, India's credit will be an instrument for disorganising her economic life. The sound policy of reserving the sterling balances for buying capital goods can not be reconciled with the Government joining the outcry against inflation. Because, deflation will stultify that policy.

But there is a greater danger of the Government deviating from the essentially sound policy of using the sterling balances to promote the industrialisation of India. In his budget speech, the Finance Member declared his readiness to abandon the plan of creating a reconstruction fund. How, then, will the sterling balances be used? Deflation will further contract the Indian market, and consumers' goods will not fetch any profit. Presumably, the new policy, not yet cleary formulated, will be to find some ways and means for transferring the sterling balances to private credit.

That will be a conspiracy against the future of India. But however powerful may be the conspirators, they are not likely to succeed. Because, unless payment is received in goods of any kind, the credit will remain indefinitely blocked. That will do no good to anybody. Therefore, India's international credit must be used up in the only possible way, namely, as public asset to serve as lever for general progress and prosperity.

The opponents of currency expansion, amply covered by the sterling balances, invoke the authority of orthodox financial doctrines. The fallacy of their position has been already exposed in the light of facts. We can now cite authority in support of our case. Criticising the "serious error in our economic thinking", which produced "absurd results", the Report of the London Chamber of Commerce says:

"The limiting factor in the production of real wealth has been the failure to distribute to would-be consumers enough money to buy the potential output. Mass production implies mass consumption. We are driven, then, to investigate the mechanism for the provision of purchasing power. While an amazing revolution has taken place in the science of production, no change, in any way commensurate, has taken place in the financial mechanism."

That is a clear verdict in favour of our contention that controlled inflation can serve the purpose of increasing purchasing power, which alone can remove the absurdities of the radically wrong economic system. Of course, it is understood that inflation can be kept under control only as a part of planned economy. Indian economy can now be planned on the basis of the sterling balances treated as a national asset which it actually is. In order to free Indian economy from the shackles of private ownership of the means of production, and private control of the channels of distribution, it is no longer necessary to risk the odium of expropriation or confiscation. The war has laid down the foundation for the economic reconstruction of India to be guided by the principle of production to meet the requirements of the community.

The possibility of putting a large amount of new money in circulation, without departing from sound financial theories and practices, will enable the Government to undertake a programme of extensive public works as part of post-war reconstruction. As soon as the war is over, thousands and thousands of motor vehicles will be available for civil transport. In order to enable Indian economy to be benefited by that windfall, old roads will have to be improved and new roads built. For that purpose, the employment of a numerous army of labour will be required. New money will remove the difficulty of footing the large wage bill. On the other hand, it will create new purchasing power.

Plentiful and cheap money will make it possible to maintain the high level of agricultural prices. That will necessitate a correspondingly high level of wages. Again there will be an increase of purchasing power. As more money in their possession will enable the peasantry to pay higher prices for manufactured goods, industrialists should not complain against higher wages and dearer raw materials. The rate of profit will fall, but greater turnover will prevent any serious decline of total profit.[2] Should the industrialists nevertheless behave unreasonably, the Government must intervene to protect and promote the welfare of the community as a whole.

---

[2] "While I am ready to admit that there is scope for improvement of our relations with labour and their conditions of work, even our strongest critic must concede that a great deal has been done during the last few years mainly through our own initiative,

Capital goods purchased for using up India's credit, treated as a national asset, will create the legal sanction for a State control of industries. Investment of public money will warrant public control to be exercised though the Government.

The import of capital goods in large quantities, not involving any cash investment, will speedily equip Indian industries for mass production. In order to avoid the absurdity of over-production, in the midst of general want, the condition for mass consumption will have to be created. Controlled inflation, again on the basis of the sterling balance, will create that condition. To build up industries to produce goods in larger and larger quantities, goods badly needed by the four hundred millions of human beings and to put money in the hands of the latter so that they can buy what they need ;—that is the solution of the problem of transforming India almost overnight from a backward country into a modern prosperous and progressive country. Planned economy can perform that miracle.

July 18, 1943.

sincerity and drive. I have however a feeling that with the sole idea of placating labour and with the hope of securing their support to the war effort, Government are forcing the pace. While we shall be prepared to consider reasonable proposals designed to meet the temporary war expediency, we strongly feel that all proposals for labour legislation of a far reaching character should be deferred for the duration of the war." (Sir Vitthal Chandavarkar's address to the annual meeting of the Millowners' Association, Bombay. 1943.)

X

PLANNED ECONOMY—III

Although Gandhist fads were incorporated in the ideals of nationalist India, as represented by the Congress, industrialisation of the country has all along been the central plank of the economic platform of nationalism. Nevertheless, the generally desired development of modern industries has been a very slow process. The political agitators hold the Government responsible for this slowness of India's economic progress. As a matter of fact, the Government has been accused of deliberately obstructing the growth of modern industries in India. There was a time when the charge was not altogether unfounded. But it is now long since the Government was compelled to abandon the earlier policy of keeping India in an industrially backward state. Just as the earlier policy was determined by the interests of British trade, just so did the policy in course of time become prejudicial to the same interests.

The British came to this country as traders, and even after they became the rulers of the country, trading here continued to be their concern. Trade is not carried on either for the purpose of harming a particular country or for endowing any blessing on it. The sole concern of the trader is to make profit. And as long as trade remains trade, there is nothing immoral or otherwise objectionable in the concern. The profit from trade with any country is, actually or potentially, limited by the latter's capacity to purchase. Therefore, it is obviously to the interest of the traders that a country with which they trade should be able to buy as much as possible. So, as soon as it became clear that India could no longer provide a progressively expanding market for British goods, to increase her purchasing power became a concern for the British traders.

It is difficult to say exactly when that point in the trade relation between the two countries was reached. As a matter of fact, the realisation of the necessity for a change in that relation could not have taken place at any point of time. It must have been a gradual process, and even that process must have affected different traders in varying degrees sooner or later. Some may still be of the opinion that no such change is necessary. Their opinion, again, is not a matter of prejudice, but of the peculiar kind of the particular branch of trade in which they are occupied. However, the point is that in course of time the economic relation between India and Britain was bound to change for the very simple reason that a static structure of Indian economy placed a limit to British trade in this country. In modern times, rehabilitation of the antiquated economic structure of any country happens in consequence of the development of power-driven industries. Therefore, in the last analysis, the charge against the British Government, to have deliberately obstructed industrialisation of the country, even in our time, has no other foundation than nationalist prejudice or political capital of the anti-British agitator.

The function of modern Imperialism provided the theoretical foundation of that charge. But on that point also, the case was often overstated, and certainly simplified by the average political agitator for whom theories are rather instruments for his purpose than scientific propositions. There is no question about it that modern Imperialism means exploitation of the backward peoples. There may be difference of opinion about the nature and extent of that exploitation. But the undeniable fact is that Imperialism obstructs the free social development of the colonial peoples. To compare the conditions of India to-day with those obtaining two-hundred years ago, is entirely beside the point. The conditions at present are certainly better than then. Only nationalist blindness would dispute this fact. But the comparison should be made with the progress made by other countries during that period. And that comparison does prove that Imperialism has prevented India from developing freely as she might have done had she been left alone. The argument that she might not have, or might indeed have fallen victim of chaotic conditions, is irrelevant. The contention is that she did not have the chance which was guaranteed to other countries by their political freedom.

To hold Imperialism responsible for anything more than that, is not theoretically permissible. The function of Imperialism was to give political protection to the privileged position of the British traders in India. Trading under the protection of modern Imperialism includes export of capital from the mother country for investment in the colonies with monopolist rights under political protection. In the beginning, that capital serves the purpose of opening up the sources of raw materials. For that purpose, the system of transport as well as a variety of industrial enterprises are necessarily developed. So, from the very beginning, trade carried on under the protection of Imperialism does contribute to the development of modern industries in the colonial countries. There is a still more fundamental consideration, which produces the same result.

Capital investment can not be profitable unless labour is exploited, and exploitation of labour takes place in the process of production. Of course, labour is employed also in the machinery of distribution. But their labour does not produce, and consequently does not serve the basic purpose of capital investment. As a matter of fact, modern Imperialism grows out of the necessity of exporting surplus capital where cheaper labour is available for production. Therefore it is not theoretically correct to hold that modern Imperialism necessarily obstructs the industrial development of colonial countries. It may do so in earlier stages. But sooner or later, the point is reached where Imperialism indeed promotes the industrialisation of the colonial countries. Refusal to do so would obviously involve the necessity of limiting the productivity of capital invested, which would be like cutting one's own nose in order to spite others'.

Instead of such absurdity, modern Imperialism would culminate in the transfer of productive industries to the periphery of the Empire, reducing the metropolis to a comfortable home of parasites, if before that it ceases to function as Imperialism. The ancient Roman Empire reached that state and collapsed under its contradictions. Therefore, modern Imperialism is not likely to make that tragic experience all over again. The germs of its dissolution are contained in its own structure. It can escape absurdities only by ceasing to be Imperialism. Subjective factors, such as repentance of the sinner, are not conditions for such development, which must take place if modern Empires are not to break down as the old Empire of the Romans, or capital invested in older colonies is not to be sent somewhere else where it can still make profit without releasing new forces of production. The latter course is blocked by the absence of new countries to be colonised.

Barring the contingency of modern civilisation collapsing, modern Empires, therefore, are bound to be internally reconstructed on the basis of changed economic relations between its different parts. Industrialisation of the colonies is indispensable for that process of reconstruction. Colonies are bound to be decolonised. Otherwise, the ideal of the liberation of the colonial people will never be realised.

The necessity for the internal reconstruction of the Empire was felt already in the earlier days of the last world war. The then Viceroy Lord Hardinge heralded the new policy to govern the relation between Britain and India by declaring that the latter must be industrialised in order to strengthen the Empire as a whole. The declaration was followed up by the appointment of the Industrial Commission which recommeded the building up of modern industries. The recommendations were not fully acted upon. Nationalism ascribed that failure to a deliberate policy on the part of the Government. One may ask why, then, was the Industrial Commission appointed, if the Government was deliberately opposed to the industrialisation of the country? It is too fatuous to argue that the object was to deceive the Indian people and the world. The fact, on the contrary, is that efforts were made to promote the growth of modern industries in the country.

To investigate the possibilities of further aid, the Fiscal Commission was appointed, and its recommendation regarding protection to Indian industries was accepted by the Government to a large extent. The none too negligible growth of the iron and steel industry is the result of the policy which was heralded by Lord Hardinge. Ever since 1924, this basic industry enjoyed a very large measure of protection not only in the form of tariff, but also subsidy. Other industries producing consumers' goods, such as textile, also enjoyed similar advantages and have considerably grown. These facts do not allow the serious student of India's economic history to lay at the door of the Government all the blame for the undoubted phenomena of her slow industrial progress. The disease is there. Only complaints would not cure it. Its causes must be detected by a searching scientific enquiry, to be removed by measures, the nature of which will also become evident in course of the same enquiry. Political agitation will not industrialise the country.

Recollection of one or two important facts will be helpful for the investigation into the cause of the slow industrial progress of India. These facts should remove the prejudice regarding the Government's responsibility in the connection. The object is not to exonerate anybody, but to create an atmosphere of objectivity which is indispensable for a scientific enquiry.

British Imperialists realised the disadvantage of keeping India in a state of industrial backwardness when, during the last war, the Indian market was very largely captured by Japan. The market for British goods was also lost to Japan, in China and other East Asiatic countries. The position could be recovered by supplying the lost markets with goods cheaper than those exported from Japan. That was possible either by seriously lowering wages in Britain, or by producing commodities in India. The British working class would not tolerate the former course. Consequently, it became advantageous for British trade in India and in other Eastern countries to build up industries in India where cheap labour was available plentifully. But capital was necessary for the purpose, and during the years immediately after the war, Britain was without any exportable surplus of capital. That was the reason for the failure to implement the new policy of Imperialism.

It is maintained by the Indian nationalists that the Government did not allow the growth of industries because they could not be built up with British capital. Why did not Indian capitalists step in? The case that they were not allowed to do so by the Government under the influence of British vested interests, is weak. The fact is that, on the contrary, the Government instituted an enquiry into India's capital resources, evidently with the purpose of mobilising them for promoting industrial production. The Banking Enquiry Committee reported that there was plenty of capital available for productive purpose. Yet, the process of industrial development could not be quickened. There must have been some other cause, deeper than those pointed out by the nationalist politicians.

The basic problem to be solved before the economic life of the country could be quickened by rapid industrialisation, was the problem of its purchasing power. Japanese goods could not simply be thrown out of the Indian market. Immediately after the war, the Indian market was flooded also by cheaper goods from European countries like Germany, Austria, Italy and Belgium. The interest of British trade, therefore, came to be to expand the Indian market. The Government was up against the basic difficulty of the low purchasing power of the bulk of the Indian people. In the last analysis, it was the problem of agrarian relations. Because, the peasantry constitutes the bulk of the Indian people. Another fact to be recollected for an objective enquiry into the economic history of contemporary India, is that the Government did try to do something for the rationalisation of India's agrarian economy. In 1925, a Royal Commission under the chairmanship of the present Viceroy was sent out to India to report on the possibilities of improving the agricultural industry. Evidently, the purpose was not purely scientific. It was to see how the purchasing power of the Indian peasantry could be increased so that the Indian market would be able to take more goods.

The recommendations of the Agricultural Commission did not help the solution of the problem of industrialisation any more than the suggestions of the Industrial, Fiscal and Banking Enquiries. It did recommend a whole series of measures for the technical improvement of agriculture; but none of them could be practised unless the peasant had some working capital. So, once again, the basic difficulty of the low purchasing power of the masses stood in the way to the efforts for an economic rehabilitation of the country. That difficulty still remains, and that is the cause of the slow industrial progress of the country. That cause must be eradicated before the generally desired industrialisation can take place. Evidently, destructive criticism of the Government's attitude or controversies about the future Constitution of India is not the right approach to the problem. The problem is economic, and it must be approached from a purely economic point of view. It is argued that Indians are not able to do so because they do not have the political power. But the argument remains without any force so long as nationalist leaders fail to say exactly how they will tackle the problem. They want industrialisation of the country. The British Government also wants the same thing. The latter has failed owing to objective difficulties. It is idle to question its *bona fides*. How do the nationalists propose to succeed where the British Government has failed? That question has not yet been answered. Consequently, all this agitation for industrialisation does not take us anywhere.

If twenty-five years ago British trade required industrialisation of India, the requirement is much greater to-day. Again, it is not necessary to go by the profession of the Government or pronouncements of individual statesmen. The economic relation between India and Britain will be determined by the economic necessities of the latter, so long as she will be ruled by a British Government. It will also be determined by the conditions of the contemporary world. The future of that relation, therefore, can be visualised from an objective analysis of Britain's post-war economic requirements and the economic conditions of the post-war world. That analysis leads to the conclusion that, for the sake of the interests of British industrialists and traders, the Government of India will find it necessary to promote the industrialisation of the country. So, a change in the political regime will make no difference as regards intention. The question is about the possibility of acting according to the intention. Until now the possibilities have been very limited. Consequently, the process of industrialisation has been slow. The British Government has failed to create new possibilities. Politics enters the picture in so far as it visualises such a Government as will conceive of new possibilities and undertake the task of creating them. Will the National Government serve the purpose?

The possibilities for the generally desired industrialisation of the country are limited by the established economic relation. Creation of new possibilities, therefore, is conditional upon a radical change, if not outright subversion, of the economic *status quo*. To put it more directly, industrialisation of India to any appreciable extent is not possible within the limits of production for exchange, that is to say, on the basis of the capitalist economy. The situation is still more aggravated by the fact that in India capitalist production itself takes place on the background of feudal and even patriarchal social relations. These relations deprive the agricultural producer practically of his entire surplus produce and consequently keep the bulk of the population on a very low standard of living which sets a rigid limit to the possibilities of the Indian market.

That is the setting of the problem of the industrialisation

of India. The problem must be therefore visualised in that setting, and only then the proper approach to it can be found. In addition to the theoretical conclusion regarding the nature of this problem, the Government's inability to do, with all its repeated efforts, what is admittedly necessary for the interests of British trade, provides the empirical support to the conclusion that the problem cannot be solved on the basis of capitalist economy. So, a change in the political regime will not be enough for promoting the economic progress of the country. The social content of that change is the decisive factor. That content can be made clear only by formulating concretely the economic programme of the National Government.

It is not an accident that, while crying hoarse for industrialisation, and blaming the Government for obstructing it deliberately, nationalist politicians have failed to present a scheme of the economic reconstruction of the country. The failure is due to their belief in *laissez faire,* the fundamental doctrine of capitalism. The National Government will only restrict import of goods from abroad by raising high tariff walls. For the rest, it will leave things as they are to-day. Assuming that consequently industries will flourish like mushrooms, what will happen to the additional commodities produced? They will have to be sold. And capitalist industrialists would not sell them except at a profit. So, India under a National Government will presently come up against the old problem of limited purchasing power of the people. That difficulty will slow down the development of industries, and who will be the scape-goat then?

It is a veritable dilemma. They only way out planned economy. The capitalist economy can not be planned. Therefore, no use of talking of industrialisation, whoever may indulge in that talk, either the British industrialists or the Indian nationalists, unless the realisation is there that it cannot be done except with the purpose of producing goods for the use of the people. Whoever will plan Indian economy from that point of view, will bring the Indian people nearer to the goal of freedom. It remains to be seen who will play that historical role.

July 25, 1943.

XI

PLANNED ECONOMY—IV

Whoever may have been responsible for retarding India's industrial progress in the past, there can no longer be any doubt about the policy Britain will adopt as regards her economic relation with India in the future. The latest evidence to that effect is Mr. Amery's speech addressing the Institute of Export on post-war trade with India. The speech can be characterised as an epoch-making pronouncement. Therefore, the more salient passages should be recorded. He said:

> "To buy from abroad goods, whether primary or manufactured, which we can produce adequately at home, by export which we might otherwise exchange for domestic production, offers no particular advantage, and may even in certain conditions result in the neglect of our own resources, natural and human, in unemployment and in the weakening of our whole economic structure. It is therefore not the gross volume, but the character of our exports and imports which is significant. There is no doubt that more and more other countries, both foreign and within the British Empire, are following and will continue to follow the policy of domestic expansion by producing for themselves many types of articles which they previously imported. I do not see in that any danger to the welfare of the world as a whole or to our own export trade, provided that we realise the new conditions, and are prepared to supply other countries with what they will in future be willing

to take from us, and not what we have been accustomed to send them in the past.

"She (India) has in her all the latent resources both of raw materials, of power and of human skill, to make her a great industrial country. To develop her own industries to the fullest possible extent, both for their own sakes and in order to raise the standard of living of her own agricultural population, is the natural and proper ambition of all patriotic Indians. Its fulfilment will no doubt involve a very considerable diversion in the character of India's import trade. It is for us not to deplore that diversion because it may affect some old established British export lines, but to be before others in recognising its character and taking full advantage of it. In the immediate post-war period, our opportunity for co-operating most effectively with Indian requirements and Indian aspirations will, no doubt, be in the provision of capital goods that India will most urgently need for industrial re-equipment and expansion. Later on, it may lie more in the provision of more specialised types of consumers' goods that the growth of India's prosperity may call for. In either case, our success will correspond directly to the extent to which our trade policy is one of whole-hearted co-operation with India's effort to raise herself on a higher plane of economic efficiency. With that wholehearted spirit of co-operation, there must also go equally wholehearted jettisoning of any lingering survival of the idea that India is, in any sense, a reserved market for British trade or for British capital. It is essential for a fresh hopeful start in the economic relations between this country and India, that there should be any vestige of the idea that in the last resort the Government of

> India's economic policy is answerable to control by the Government of the United Kingdom, or that British firms or British goods have behind them any other backing than that which they would receive from their Government in any other country. It is by their own merit that they must stand or fall. They can yet, in the prosperous and expanding Indian economy, increasingly share in that expansion to India's true benefit and their own."

The full implication of this pronouncement can not be appreciated by those who interject psychology into economics. Imperialism is a thing of the past, whether the Imperialists like it or not. The fact is that they are themselves singing the swan song of Imperialism. Nobody is going to be de-colonised because to keep her in the backward state of colonial economy has ceased to be a profitable business. The de-colonisation of India will not economically harm Britain. As Mr. Amery himself admitted, continuation of Imperialism would mean "neglect of our own resources" and consequently weaken "our whole economic structure."

The war will leave the British Government heavily indebted to India. How will payment be made? That post-war problem is bound to determine Britain's economic policy towards India. There cannot be any question about Britain's willingness to respect her obligations. So, the nationalist doubt about Britain's *bona fides* is all groundless, and may even be the reflexion of what one would do in the same position. International trade is built on credit. Therefore, nobody willingly gambles with the asset. Moreover, ultimately more will be gained by paying the debt than by repudiating it. The payment will mean a large volume of trade which will bring considerable profit.

The time-honoured dictum that honesty is the best policy has foundation of long experience.

Payments are proposed to be made in goods. Nationalists seem to object to that. They would like to receive payment in gold. But that only indicates backwardness of their economic ideas. If gold was received in payment, they would not know what to do with it, and it would be a white elephant for Indian economy. Prosperity of a nation is no longer measured by the weight of ornaments worn by the ladies of the upper classes. But in reality the nationalists do not want India's international credit to be frozen into bricks of gold. They want the sterling balances to be converted into dollar securities, so that India may not be compelled to buy only in Britain. So, in the last analysis, India must receive payment in goods, whether from Britain or any other country. It is quite legitimate for Britain to insist that the goods should be taken from her. Her indebtedness to India is the result of her having purchased goods from India. Why should she not be allowed to pay in kind? And what will be the harm for India if she buys from Britain the goods she will need? Her right is to decide what kind of goods she will take. Britain is no longer disputing that right. Indeed, she is anxious to pay in exactly the kind of goods that India should take for her own welfare. This identity of interest will determine British economic policy towards India, and the outlines of that policy are drawn by Mr. Amery in his speech.

The payment must be made mostly in capital goods, because immediately India will not be able to take any considerable amount of consumers' goods. If it was to the interests of British trade to obstruct the industrialisation of India, Britain could withhold payment instead of paying in capital goods. But eventually British industry will have to be shifted back to the production of consumers' goods, and thanks to the tremendous expansion and technological improvement during the war, will be producing consumers' goods in a much larger quantity. A part of them will have to be exported. Consequently, increase of the purchasing power of the backward countries has become a condition for the economic reconstruction of the world after the war. By paying her debt to India, through the export of capital goods, Britain will do good business immediately, and lay the foundation for better business in the future. Industrialisation of India will revolutionise Indian economy and increase her purchasing power. It may be doubted whether the policy is really so farsighted. But again it is not a matter of choice. It is like a forced move in a game of chess. And the result will be no defeat or discredit for any body, but gain for all.

Unfortunately for the future of Indo-British relations, British statesmen, and particularly Mr. Amery, have a bad reputation in this country. He may speak God's own truth, yet the nationalists would be suspicious. But on this occasion Mr. Amery has not spoken as an individual.[1] Those who have carefully followed the development of economic thought in British business circles, know that the opinion expressed by him has crystallised in course of a searching investigation into the problems of Post-War

---

[1] "It is essential for a fresh hopeful start in the economic relations between this country and India that there should be no vestige of the idea that in the last resort the Government of India's economic policy is answerable to control by the Government of the United Kingdom or that the British firms or the British goods have behind them any other backing than that which they would receive from their Government in any other country, whether within or without the British Commonwealth. It is by their own merits that they should stand or fall." (Mr. L. S. Amery—Address to the Institute of Export, *Times of India*, July 19, 1943.)

Reconstruction. He has simply endorsed the revolutionary findings of the Special Committee of the London Chamber of Commerce which investigated the problems of post-war reconstruction. The findings, in substance, were that Imperialism must go if the economic absurdities which characterised the period between the two wars, and prepared the ground for this war, were not to be repeated. It is only a dramatic gesture to have the swan song of Imperialism sung by one who has earned the reputation of being the most die-hard Imperialist. We do not know if Mr. Amery's speech was so stage-managed. But it is evident that he trimmed his sail according to the wind and that certainly is wise statesmanship.

To be convinced that Mr. Amery was not fooling India or hood-winking the world, and to realise the fullest implications of his pronouncement, it is necessary to recollect the findings of the London Chamber of Commerce, and its basic recommendations.

> "The limiting factor in the production of real wealth has been the failure to distribute to would-be consumers enough money to buy the potential output and that goods are not for long produced if there are no buyers. Mass production implies mass consumption. We are driven then to investigate the mechanism for the provision of purchasing power.
>
> "Instead of trying to equate supply with effective demand the Chamber advocate that in future effective demand should be equated with supply. There can be no such thing as general over-production of which complaint was made after the last war. The real trouble is under-consumption."

The recommendation is:

> "The distribution internally of the purchasing power

> necessary to enable the nations to consume the whole of their own production ; if this were done, they could equally consume the goods of other nations which they might exchange for their own production."

It is obvious that Mr. Amery's speech indicates how reconstruction of British economy as recommended by the London Chamber of Commerce will influence the economic relation between Britain and India. So, it can be safely assumed that, as soon as the war will be over, capital goods necessary for the building up of a modern industry will be available to India. As no payment will have to be made, and Britain will be eager to export goods, it will be all a matter only of transportation. The huge amount of sterling balances will enable India to import capital goods almost in unlimited quantity. What will be the consequence of that apparently favourable position ?

The coveted ideal of industrialisation will be attained. But industries are not built for fun. Much larger quantities of goods will be produced than previously. Mass production, however, is not a blessing by itself. It requires mass consumption. Who will buy the increased products of new Indian industries? Before long, India will experience "the absurdity of over-production," while the bulk of the people will still remain underfed, ill-clothed and without practically all other amenities of life. It is this problem of restricted purchasing power of the masses which really arrested the industrialisation of India in the past. It will do so also in the future, even when British Imperialism will no longer be the devil of the drama. Without a solution of that basic problem, industrialisation of India is not possible. If India is to be benefited by the revolutionary consequences of this war, her post-war economy must be planned.

Had the decisive factor of the restricted purchasing power of the masses been in operation, nothing could have prevented Indian capitalists to build up modern industries, even when British Imperialism was opposed to it. Capital goods could be always purchased, if not from Britain, from other countries. If British ships would not be available for carrying them, there were others who would be only too glad to have the trade. The Government of India never prohibited import of capital goods, nor imposed prohibitive customs duties. Nevertheless industries did not grow.

A National Goverment, therefore, would not be able to create any more favourable conditions than are already available, thanks to the exigencies of post-war reconstruction of the world. It will be able to do one thing which is coveted by the Indian capitalist, and that is the only privilege that they could not secure from the Imperailist Government. Protection was given to the basic Iron and Steel Industry, and to a number of other subsidiary industries. But that did not help much. Indian capitalists wanted the Government to adopt the Japanese practise of subsidising the export of manufactured commodities. In that case, Indian industries could grow without having to face the problem of increasing the purchasing power of the Indian masses. But that practise would hardly be helpful after this war. Because there will be a much keener competition for the world market. Moreover, under all circumstances the basic condition of the industrialisation of the country, in our time, is the progressive expansion of the internal market. Foreign market is not a reliable factor.

The condition can be created in India. The Indian market is potentially unlimited. The only thing to be done is to convert human demand into effective demand. In other words, to distribute purchasing power to the millions who badly need all sorts of manufactured commodities. The position is as follows : India can consume vast quantities of manufactured goods, but even a small fraction of them can not be sold at a profit. The conclusion is obvious. Industrialisation of India is possible only if production will be for use. In other words, on the basis of capitalist economy, that is, production for profit, industrialisation of India is not possible. This difficulty will not be removed even by the benefit of India having built up a vast international credit during the war. As a matter of fact, that benefit will not be available to her, unless industries will be built with the purpose of producing goods for use. Only then Indian economy can be planned, and the absurdity of over-production in an atmosphere of general want, can be avoided.

It is comparatively easy to estimate how much consumers' goods will be necessary to supply the Indian people so as to guarantee them a human standard of living. Having done that, industries will be built to meet the requirement. It can be easily imagined that the initial programme of industrialisation will be necessarily quite substantial. The present industries can supply only a very small part of the minimum needs of the people. Since the new industries will be financed out of the national asset in the form of the sterling balances in London, the question of profit should not present any difficulty. Of course, it will not be manufacturing goods and simply giving them away. What is necessary is to fix prices low enough so as to bring the commodities within the actual purchasing power of the bulk of the population. Even that will leave a narrow margin of profit, if the industries are not burdened with other charges such as interest on capital, sinking funds, high dividends and innumerable others usual in private concerns.

But that is only the beginning. The position will not be very sound. The next step is to increase the purchasing power of the masses. The first step in that direction will result from the building of new industries and the general expansion of industrial production. Because, more labour will be employed, and some more purchasing power will be distributed in the form of additional wages. On the other hand, withdrawal of some labour from the overburdened agriculture will correspondingly improve the level of agricultural wages, amounting to some more purchasing power. But to place the newly created industries on a sounder economic basis, the increase of purchasing power cannot be left to take care of itself. Measures must be taken to quicken it. One of them will be creation of new employment. Industrial employment will not increase substantially until the purchasing power of the peasant masses increases considerably. That will require radical readjustment of the relation of property in land. Meanwhile, an extensive public works programme will create a good deal of new employment. That programme can also be financed out of the national asset. It can be so extensive as to give employment to several million workers. The wages paid to them will create new purchasing power.

Controlled inflation of currency will be another measure for increasing purchasing power. It will not be necessary to issue more currency notes than in circulation to-day. What will be necessary is to see that they are really in circulation. At present the great bulk of it is locked up in banks or being used for speculative purposes. Very little of it enters into the exchange of commodities. By keeping the agricultural prices on a reasonably high level, and taking measures to guarantee that the benefit goes actually to the primary producer, money will be very widely distributed, increasing the purchasing power of the peasant masses. The present possibility of selling manufactured commodities worth approximately five hundred crores of rupees offers a very broad foundation to Indian industries. What is necessary, is to make a reality out of that possibility. Then, so long as the Reserve Bank holds its present securities, it will be quite a sound financial practice to issue twice as many currency notes as are in circulation to-day. Only a small fraction of the sterling balances has been transferred to the Issue Department of the Reserve Bank to cover the currency. So, controlled inflation will double the present potential purchasing power.

Finally, the basic problem of the economic life of the country will have to be tackled. It is the problem of the antiquated, unproductive, relations in the property of land, which still is the main means of production. Agriculture being the principal industry of the country, the major portion of national wealth is created by it. The value of total income from agriculture has not been estimated. But the value of the share of those who own the land, but do not contribute anything to the process of agricultural production, has been approximately estimated. In view of the economic bankruptcy of the bulk of the peasantry, that share should be regarded as the net income from agricultural industry. A good many landowners are also economically bankrupt. Their income does not represent saving. Nevertheless, the major portion of the total income of the landowning class goes to a small minority of that class. The justification of surplus production, represented by net national income, is that it serves as the lever for expanding production. Therefore, it is quite fair as well as economically sound position that the net income from the main industry of the the country should be more widely distributed so as to increase the purchasing power of the masses, thus broadening the foundation for the industrialisation of the country.

The socially necessary readjustment of the relations of property in land, transfer of the ownership from a non-producing class to the actual producer, may not be included in the plan of India's economic reconstruction immediately after the war. The initial part of the plan will work out successfully if the burden on the peasantry (rents, interests and the innumerable other feudal and semi-feudal levies) is reduced at the cost of the small class of landowners at present appropriating the bulk of the net agricultural income. If not more than fifteen per cent of his net income is taken away from the peasant, the economic condition of the peasantry will appreciably improve. There will be new purchasing power amounting to perhaps more than a hundred crores of rupees. Fitted into the scheme of controlled inflation, the net increase of the peasant's income will be much more in current money value.

All these measures together can be expected to increase the purchasing power of the country by two or three hundred per cent. Industrialisation of the country at a sufficiently rapid tempo will be a practical possibility. The obstacle to that economic progress, now within the reach of India, is insistence upon the capitalist mode of production with its doctrine of *laissez faire.* This doctrine will not permit any one of the above measures. As a matter of fact, it is antagonistic to the very idea of planning economy. The war has created conditions which will enable India to overcome that obstacle. She only needs to use her national asset to promote public welfare.

Concretely, the sterling balances should be treated as national asset; they should be used, in the first place, for purchasing capital goods, and in the second place, to provide cover for a controlled inflation of currency; industries financed out of the national asset should not be owned privately, or run by private profit motive ; they should produce in order to meet the estimated needs of the people. The Government, at the same time, should introduce measures which will enable the masses to buy the manufactured commodities they need; finally, the basic problem of land-ownership should be tackled so that agriculture could be rationalised through the introduction of machinery, which will increase agricultural production while considerably reducing labour performed on land.

Planned industrial production for use must have its own channel of distribution. Private trade will have to be supplemented by organisation for co-operative buying and selling. Direct connection between the producers and consumers will make planning easier. Evidently, the welfare of the Indian people as well as the solution of the problem of the post-war reconstruction of the world demand that India should have a Government which will be free to plan her economy on the above lines.

August 1, 1943.

APPENDIX A

MEMORANDUM ON THE DISTRIBUTION OF FOOD AND OTHER NECESSITIES

Submitted to H. E. the Viceroy, on January 9, 1943

1. Soon after the creation of the Department of Food Supply of the Government of India, I took the liberty of addressing a letter to the Hon'ble Member in charge, making a few suggestions regarding the methods to be adopted for tackling the problem.

2. In addition to the extensive experience of the two popular organisations, with which I am connected, namely, the Indian Federation of Labour and the Radical Democratic Party, the Hon'ble Commerce Member's address to the Sixth Price Control Conference was the basis of my suggestions.

3. There has been, and still there is, a good deal of confusion and perhaps wilful misrepresentation, about the cause of the scarcity of food and other elementary necessities. Consequently, the Government seem to have been misguided, and all efforts for coping with the situation have until now proved ineffective.

4. The nature of the problem was very correctly defined by the Hon'ble Commerce Member in his address to the Sixth Price Control Conference. It is a problem of distribution. The scarcity is artificially created. The demand for a ban on export is evidently made with the purpose of concealing the real issue. The present export is practically negligible. Therefore, its stoppage would not help the situation substantially. There is convincing statistical evidence to the effect that the stock in the country is enough to meet all requirements. There has been no serious crop failure, nor has there been any substantial displacement of labour from agriculture to other industries. Therefore, the Hon'ble Commerce Member was perfectly right in saying that it was a problem of distribution.

5. The approach to the problem, however, has not been such as is clearly called for by its admitted nature. The problem of distribution of scarcity in the midst of plenty could be created only by a breakdown of the existing machinery of distribution. As a matter of fact, it has not been a case of breakdown. but wilful obstruction, motivated very largely politically. The present crisis has been precipitated as a different, more effective, form of the recent sabotage movement which failed to attain its object.

6. Having visualised the problem in the light of the political situation of the country, I made the following suggestion in my letter to the Hon'ble Commerce Member, dated November 26, 1942:

"The creation of a machinery to guarantee free distribution of foodstuff and other primary necessities is the need of the moment. It is now evident that no measure of control can keep the prices down and guarantee a free supply, so long as the normal channels of trade are regarded as the only machinery of distribution available or conceivable. As a matter of fact, the problem of food supply is created by obstacles which profit-motive places in the channels of a free distribution of commodities through trade. Profiteering is clearly a trader's practice. Hoarding is also done by traders in this country; because the vast bulk of consumers are too poor to hoard. Therefore, the conclusion is irresistable that the problem of distribution cannot be solved unless there will be another machinery. The newly created Department of Food Supply will not contribute much to the solution of the problem, unless it applies itself to this task.

"It is reported that the new Department may serve the purpose of the Central Government purchasing the entire stock of basic foodstuffs, such as wheat, and then distribute it equitably through the normal channels of trade, which will, of course, be subjected to certain measures of control. If the purchase is made directly from the producer, the latter may be benefited in the form of getting the higher price fixed by the government. But the consumer cannot be expected to be any better off than at present, because the supply available to him will be still at the mercy of the traders.

"The Government entering into trade may be too drastic a measure. But there is a middle way. It is rapid development of consumers' co-operative societies with the acid, and under the patronage of the government. That will serve as an alternative machinery for distribution. By itself, it will render a good deal of assistance to the consumers. On the other hand, by acting as a check, it will make the normal channels of trade more amenable to measures of control.

"Although the beginning should be made with consumers' co-operatives, before long small producers should be also helped to sell their produce through co-operative organisations.

"If these proposals are generally accepted, then the details could be easily worked out in consultation with the various parties concerned and on the basis of the experience made by public workers who have been trying to contribute to the solution of the problem of food supply."

7. Since the above was written, the situation has aggravated into a veritable crisis which may seriously disturb public peace and order. It would be unwise for the authorities to disregard

the presence of agencies anxious to exploit the situation for their political purposes. The authorities would be well advised to face the fact that there is a connection between the cause of the present crisis and those mischeivious agencies. Therefore, all other efforts having failed, the Government should now at least fall back on the suggestion of creating an alternative machinery of distribution with the active co-operation of the mass of consumers. In order to be fully effective the machinery of distribution should be supplemented by co-operative marketing societies. Through this method, the Government will not only solve the problem of supply of food and other primary necessities but will at the same time establish an abiding practical relationship which will bridge the deplorable gulf between itself and the people.

8. The Indian Federation of Labour and the Radical Democratic Party have all along concerned themselves with the question of the supply of food and other primary necessities, and tried to help the authorities in making them available to the poor consumers at controlled prices. The All-India Conference of the Radical Democratic Party held at Lucknow from December 25 to 27, 1942, considered the present crisis and resolved to organise popular initiative for helping the Government to overcome it. The Executive Committee of the Indian Federation of Labour also met on the same occasion. Both these popular organisations have resolved to organise consumers' co-operatives and marketing societies throughout the country. Having a far-flung network of organisations, and an army of selfless public workers, they are in a position to do so. But the essential condition for the success of their efforts is co-operation from the side of the authorities in the form of placing supplies at the disposal of the co-operative societies, and of credit facilities.

9. In behalf of the two popular organisations, which have uncompromisingly supported the efforts of the Government, and are sincerely anxious to establish a close relation between the Government and the people as the basis for the economic welfare and political progress of the country, I appeal for an unreserved acceptance of their co-operation for overcoming the crisis precipitated by the conspiracy of powerful anti-social elements. The newly created department of Food Supply can be the medium of that co-operation. In order to serve that purpose, it must be an independent department in charge of a man who would feel the necessity and have the courage to go out of the beaten track, and adopt measures which will certainly not be approved by the commercial community, which cannot be absolved of the responsibility for having precipitated the present crisis.

10. It was not proper to associate the Department of Food Supply with the Department of Commerce. If the problem of supply could be solved through the normal channels of trade it would not be necessary for the Government to create a new department for interfering in the process. On the other hand if the

necessity for such interference is felt, that cannot be done effectively strictly within the framework of private trade.

11. It is admitted by the Hon'ble Commerce Member that the measures of control have not produced the desired result. Much is being made of this admission by interested parties. If this admission leads to a reversal to the policy of *laissez faire*, as persistently demanded by the commercial community, the situation will further aggravate. And the dangers resulting therefrom can be easily imagined.

12. Any effective control of prices presupposes control of the stock. Therefore, no measure of control will be effective unless the problem is tackled at the root. The Government must take over the entire available stock of all primary necessities, and arrange for its distribution through a new machinery beyond the control of those who have either conspired to bring about the present situation, or have failed to prevent it. Immediately, strong measures should be adopted for dealing with hoarders and profiteers. The stock held by them should be taken over by the Government and handed over to the co-operative societies on credit to be distributed at the controlled price. Active co-operation of the Indian Federation of Labour and the Radical Democratic Party and any other popular organisation taking up a similar attitude, should be welcomed by local authorities to search out hidden stores. Popular vigilance corps should be organised with that purpose. Local authorities should give all help and encouragement for the organisation of those bodies.

13. Generally, the Government or India should be immediately reconstituted with the inclusion of men with organized popular support, and therefore will be guided rather by the consideration of general welfare than concern for sectional interests. It is highly deplorable that no representative of organised labour has found a place in the Government of India. It is equally deplorable that the only political party of the people, which has unconditionally supported the war and stood by the Government when it was being stabbed in the back, is not taken into confidence. On the other hand, representatives of trade and industry as well as of the land-owning interest are allowed to bungle the situation, even when the Government can have the confidence and support of the popular masses only for the asking.

14. The Indian Federation of Labour and the Radical Democratic Party keenly feel that all their efforts to bridge the gulf between the Government and the people will be frustrated if the Government will remain under the sectional interests which necessarily prevent it from adopting a popular policy.

Dehradun, January, 9, 1943.

APPENDIX B

A COSTLY EXPERIMENT: PRIVATE TRADE FINANCED WITH PUBLIC MONEY

Statement issued by the Central Executive Committee of the Radical Democratic Party on April 25, 1943.

The declaration made by the Additional Secretary of the Government of India in the Food Department, in his recent radio talk, that hoarders and profiteers would be firmly dealt with, is welcome. But experience does not inspire the belief that this threat will have any more salutary effect than that made by the Finance Member in his speech concluding the Budget Debate in the Central Legislative Assembly. It is not likely to be anything more serious than another stage thunder to draw applause from the credulous; it may be also meant to hide the shame of defeat which, however, is rather due to the pusillanimity on the part of the Government than to the cleverness of the enemy. It was a pusillanimity not only in dealing with those brazenly engaged in anti-social practices, but also in compelling lower officials to enforce the orders of the Government.

Notwithstanding the war-like language of the official exponent of the policy, it is an abject surrender to the enemies of the people, those who are conspiring with the typically fascist method of starving the people so that, in utter despair, the latter may lend themselves as pawns in the political game of the privileged few aspiring for dictatorial power.

Indeed, the Government has not only capitulated to the public enemy; it has undertaken also to pay a heavy indemnity. The removal of ineffective control, ineffective because it was not enforced, will now be followed up with the costly experiment of financing private trade with public money.

The policy is presented as a long term programme. It has been declared that the Government of India has assured adequate food supply for all the provinces and States for the next twelve months. That is certainly a heartening declaration. But the laudable concern for a long term programme should not minimise the importance of immediate measures to relieve the hardships of the people. There has been negligence on that score. Since the Food Department of the Government of India was created, and began functioning by abolishing all control on prices, the food situation has aggravated. The hope that the removal of control on prices will bring hoarded stocks in the market has not been fulfilled. The price level in the wholesale market may have shown some tendency to decline slightly. But what concerns the vast bulk of the consumers is the retail price, which they actually have to pay. And it is a challenging fact that, since the abolition of control, retail prices have not fallen; on the contrary, they not only have risen, but there has been little relief of the artificially created scarcity.

These deplorable facts place the stamp of failure on the initial stage of the Government of India's new food policy. The second part of the plan, now announced being only a continuation of the first, cannot be expected to produce any better result.

The guiding principle of the policy is to rely on normal commecial methods; there will be no control whatsoever. This reversal to the time-honoured doctrine of *laissez-faire* is expected to guarantee fair prices both to the producer and the consumer. Evidently, there is a fallacy in the argument. Control was introduced only when, during the first two and half years of the war, prices kept on soaring without any tangible reason. So, it is a matter of experience that *laissez-faire* did not produce the result which it is expected to produce now. In the past, prices rose when there was no control on normal commercial methods. Where, then, is the guarantee that in the future prices will fall in consequence of all control on the normal commercial methods being removed?

The operative part of the plan is that the Central Government will purchase the entire surplus of food grains and distribute it to the deficit areas. It is announced that more than one hundred crores of rupees will be required to execute this part of the plan. That would be a step in the right direction. When the price control was introduced, we maintained that it could not succeed unless the Government took over the control of the stocks. Now the Government proposes to do so, having first abandoned the policy of price control. But it believes that the very fact of the Government securing the surplus will serve as a control on price. That might be so if the surplus was not to be acquired through private traders, and brought to the market also though the private traders. But the Government has decided to spend one hundred crores of rupees to finance private trade, to enable a selected few to buy cheap and sell dear. That, after all, is the essence of trade.

The Government disclaims any intention of putting anybody out of business. There will be no control on normal commercial methods. Evidently, there is a good deal of confused thinking, if not actual desire to connive with the malpractices of anti-social elements. That is clear from the answer to the simple question: What is trade? Is it not simply to buy cheap and sell dear? Why should methods devised for attaining that object be considered indispensable for guaranteeing a free flow of essential commodities from the producer to the consumer? Trade is considered to be normal (by the traders) when commodities could be bought at the lowest price and sold at the highest. Evidently, non-interference with the normal commercial methods will not produce the result of bringing down price. And as prices could be forced up by withholding goods from the consumers, the artificially created scarcity will continue, and there will be no alleviation of the crisis which is causing untold misery and endless hardships for the vast bulk of the population.

The Government of India will secure control of the surplus through the agency of the Provincial and State Governments. The actual purchasing will be done by commercial firms empowered to do so by the respective Provincial and State Governments. So, for all practical purposes, the surplus will remain under the control of private traders even after the Government of India has invested a large amount of public money. As there will be no control anywhere, the producers will have to accept whatever price will be offered by the privileged firms carrying on trade with the financial assistance of the Government.

The distribution of the surplus to the deficit provinces and States will presumably take place also through normal commercial channels. The traders actually holding the surplus stock purchased with public money will sell to the needy Provinces and States Again, there will be no control on the prices they will be pleased to demand. The price paid by the deficit provinces and States in getting their quota of the surplus through private traders will naturally determine the rate of price the consumers will have to pay ultimately. The food grains originally purchased with public money will have to pass through the hands of another set of traders before they will reach the hungry mouths of the consumers. Having received their quota of the surplus through private traders, the Provincial and State Governments will hand it over to another set of traders for bringing them in the market. In the absence of any control, there will be nothing to prevent them from charging any price they like.

Thus, legal control of the surplus will not enable the Government to use it so as to keep prices approximately on a certain level. In order to produce that result, the surplus must operate as a competitive factor. It cannot do so when it will reach the consumers through the normal channels of tade. A trader is not likely to sell commodities purchased with Government money cheaper than those purchased with his own money. If he did, he would not be a trader.

The decisive question is: how will the surplus purchased by the Government reach the consumers? If it cannot flow through a channel other than the so-called normal trade, then it can never be "the deluge of grain" which will crush the speculator. The Government's plan provides no guarantee against the surplus itself being cornered instead of breaking the speculators' conspiracy.

The Government has adopted such a palpably impractical policy, becaue it still refuses to approach the problem from the right angle of vision. An economic crisis, pregnant of grave consequences, has been brought about by a political conspiracy. The

Government still believes that hoarding, profiteering and black market were all caused by lack of confidence, fear and uncertainty. Now that an improvement in the military position of India has taken place, it is expected that the causes will disappear, and consequently hoarders, profiteers and speculators will also disappear as nightmares of yesterday. That is wishful thinking, if not worse. Precisely because the military situation has improved, the enemy has decided to attack on a different front. It should be remembered that the food situation has deteriorated rapidly during this year since the Japs stopped on the Eastern frontiers of India. It being thus essentially a political problem, the approach should also be political. But the Government persistently avoids a political approach, and blissfully regards the problem as a simple economic problem which can be solved by a reversal to the good old method of *laissez-faire*. It is only common sense that, if you let your enemy do whatever he likes, on the ground that Government interference with trade is not desirable, you only undermine your own position. The danger is palpable. Food riots are already reported from different places. If the hardships are not relieved soon, they may become wide-spread. It is very easy to incite a hungry mob, with no prospect of any relief, to desperate action.

The situation being so very fraught with danger, it is necessary for the Government to act with boldness. Its hands should not be bound by prejudices and conventional notions. There is absolutely no reason why the Government should not go into business, particularly when private businessmen are engaged in an economic hold-up. Moreover, it is no use doing things half and half. According to its new policy, the Government will invest a large sum of money for purchasing food grains. So, it is going into business Why, then, still let private traders derive the benefit of being financed by the public Exchequer, and also frustrate the good intentions of the Government? Let the Government take over the surplus of food grains directly from the producer, thus guaranteeing him a fair price, and then create a parallel channel through which the surplus will reach the consumers directly. Private traders being eliminated from the entire process, a really fair price will thus be guaranteed also to the consumers.

The objection to the Government going into business is that it will involve bureaucratic practices. Assuming that will be so, there will be nothing new. Until now, the net result of the Government's food policy has been to expand a bureaucratic machinery. It has not only been ineffective, but much worse. It has not been above corruption. Even the new policy, while leaving the field free to private traders, will create a bureaucratic machinery which will have very little to do. Therefore, the argument against the Government directly intervening in the process of primary necessities flowing freely from the producers to the consumers, is unconvincing.

But it is not necessary for the Government to go into business itself. What it needs do is to help the opening of a parallel channel for the surplus, purchased with public money, to flow directly from the producer to the consumer. Co-operative Marketing Societies at the one end, and Consumers' Co-operatives, on the other, will open up that parallel channel. Let the Government declare that the surplus taken over by it will be distributed only through the Consumers' Co-operative Societies, and let it make it a point to purchase the surplus through the Co-operative organisations of the primary produccers. In no time, these co-operative organisatios, of the producer on the one end, and of the consumer, in the other, will grow and become a decisive factor in the economic life of the country. Only then, the surplus purchased by the Government will operate as a competitive factor. Through the new channel, grain from the surplus store will flow wherever there will be a scarcity owing to speculation or cornering. It easy to see what will be the result. Not only black markets will disappear because they will cease to be profitable ; the political game of the hoarders and profiteers will also be up, because the new channel of distribution will put an end to artificially created scarcity. Consequently, prices will come down to the level which will have to be maintained for guaranteeing a fair return to the producer.

The Government has failed to find this obvious and practical solution of the problem, because neither the masses of small producers nor of poor consumers enter anywhere into its calculations. It cannot think except in terms of trade and traders. Let the concern for the vested interest of the fortunate few, most of whom are engaged in anti-social practices, be replaced by a genuine concern for the welfare of the people, and the Government will find itself out of the present highly explosive situation. The food question concerns primarily the masses of the poor people. They constitute the majority of the nation. Democratic practice must be determined by the voice of the majority. Let the majority assert itself, and all the problems will be solved.

APPENDIX C

TABLE NO. 1.

Index numbers of (1) Monetary Circulation, (2) Wholesale Prices (Calcutta) and (3) Cost of Living (Bombay)

	Note Circulation	Wholesale Prices	Cost of Living
1939			
July	100	100	100
August	99	100	100
September	108	114	101
October	116	118	103
November ...	121	131	104
December	127	137	108
1940			
January	131	130	109
February	133	125	107
March	133	121	105
April	133	121	105
May	135	117	106
June	138	114	106
July	134	114	108
August	130	115	109
September	128	119	107
October	128	121	108
November	127	122	108
December	130	120	110

TABLE NO. 1.—(*Contd.*)

	Note Circulation	Wholesale Prices	Cost of Living
1941			
January	135	121	111
February	138	119	118
March	141	123	118
April ...	147	127	115
May	150	130	116
June	150	137	116
July	150	159	120
August	150	151	125
September	157	149	123
October	161	151	119
November	167	157	129
December	180	154	123
1942			
January	198	155	131
February	205	158	129
March	221	158	130
April	237	157	131
May	251	169	135
June	242	182	145
July	248	182	160

TABLE NO. 1.—(*Contd.*)

			Note Circulation	Wholesale Prices	Cost of Living
1942					
August	...	...	258	192	160
September	...	...	269	198	162
October	...	...	280	209	164
November	...	...	295	227	170
December	...	...	309	238	179
1943					
January	..	...	324	250	193
February	...	..	336	253	195
March	...	...	350	272	198
April	...	...	367	293	214
May	...	...	384	325	216
June	...	...	397	319	{221 {224
July	...	..	406	332	225
August	...	...	415	345	227
September	...	...	419	349	233
October	...	...	427	334	236
November	...	...	437	314	...

*The figures for Bombay up to May June 1943, relate to the month ending 15th and those from June 1943, relate to a Calender Month.

TABLE NO. 2.

INDEX NUMBERS OF WHOLESALE PRICES IN INDIA BY GROUPS OF COMMODITIES.

Year and Month		Food and Tobacco	Other agricultural commodities	Raw materials	All primary commodities	Manufactured articles	Chief articles of export	General index
1939-40								
August	...	100·3	100·7	100·2	100·3	100·0	100·6	100·3
December	...	127·1	187·1	129·3	136·5	14·51	147·9	138·3
March	...	117·9	151·5	125·4	125·9	133·0	131·5	127·5
1940-41								
April	...	112·7	157 9	122 8	123·2	131·5	128·2	125 0
May	..	109·6	135·9	123·4	119·0	127·3	162·4	120·8
June	...	103·5	112·8	112 2	108·3	117·1	107·3	110·3
July	...	106·5	110 4	118 4	111·6	113·5	110·8	112·1
August	...	103·2	98·2	118·9	108·1	109·3	106·3	108·4
September	...	107·6	107·1	116·9	111·0	111 4	109·7	111·1
October	...	109·6	100·2	120 2	111·3	112·9	111·0	112·1
November	..	109·1	106 4	125·6	114 8	118·9	115·9	115·7
December	...	107·8	102·5	124·0	112 9	119·8	114·2	114·4
January	...	107 4	99·6	126 3	112·9	121·6	114·3	11·48
February	...	103·6	94 5	121·1	108·4	121·5	107·9	111·1
March	...	108 1	112 4	125·9	115·4	131·7	116·7	118·8
1941-42								
April	...	103·5	103·2	128·6	112·6	131·5	113·2	116·4
May	...	104·6	121·0	130·9	116·9	139·7	121·4	121·5
June	...	114·7	128·7	139·0	126·0	146·7	132·7	130·2
July	..	127 0	142·2	146 2	136·7	157·3	145·1	140·9
August	...	128 6	152 7	147 2	139·4	161 2	148·0	142·5
September	...	125·8	141 6	145 8	135·9	167·3	145·2	142 2
October	...	126·6	134 6	150·5	136 8	163 0	145·0	142·1
November	...	128 6	146·3	156·1	141·7	165·3	148·9	146·5
December	...	127 1	137·5	150 0	137·5	153 8	139·0	140·0
January	...	130·6	129 9	158 4	141 7	161·4	143·0	145·0
February	...	133 7	123·0	157·9	141·7	163·3	142·4	145·1
March	...	132·9	117·4	161·9	140·6	165·2	139·7	145·6
1942-43								
April	...	138 5	114 8	162·4	142·8	157·6	138·9	145·9
May	...	144 9	123·2	160·1	146·7	162·6	141·3	149·9
June	...	160 2	135 8	161·4	150·3	167·4	151·5	158·6

TABLE NO. 2.—(*Contd.*)

Year and Month		Food and Tobacco	Other agricultural commodities	Raw materials	All primary commodities	Manufactured articles	Chief articles of export	General Index
July	...	155·5	148·7	163·5	157·4	175·6	153·3	161·2
August	...	260·2	141·6	161·8	157·5	174·6	152·3	161·1
September	...	164·1	159·7	164·0	163·3	182·3	156·7	167·3
October	...	169·9	178·8	166·3	169·9	194·4	165·9	175·0
November	...	173·6	179·5	171·0	173·6	220·0	170·3	182·7
December	...	181·1	178·2	172·0	177·0	222·2	171·8	186·0
January	...	201·5	193·8	171·5	188·0	225·8	185·5	195.6
February	...	211·9	202·5	172·0	193·9	225·3	191·4	200·4
March	...	271·0	212·3	172·0	218·0	227·9	220·5	220·1
1943								
April	..	285·4	240·1	172·9	228·2	239·4	234·4	230·5
May	...	299·0	243·2	174·8	234·4	250·0	241·6	237·8
June	...	303·0	238·5	182·1	238·8	263·5	243·1	244·0
July	...	295·0	226·2	186·2	236·0	259·6	239·3	240·9
August	...	300·2	206·2	181·4	231·8	252·3	237·4	236·1
September	...	302·6	220·4	183·8	236·3	253·4	243·3	240·0
October	...	303·0	219·6	185·4	237·1	257·6	244·1	241·5
November	...	301·1	199·8	189·3	234·8	253·3	238·9	238·7

(**Base:** 19th August 1939—100; **Source:** Economic Adviser to The Government of India.)

TABLE NO. 3.

The following is the relevant statistical material regarding Notes in Circulation, and Gold Coin and Bullion, Sterling Securities, Rupee Coin, and the Rupee Securities in the Issue Department of The Reserve Bank of India.

(In lakhs of Rupees)

	Notes in Circulation	Gold Coin & Bullion	Sterling Securities	Rupee Coin	Rupee Securities
Annual Average:					
1935-36 .. .	16,406	4,442	6.209	5.551	2,962
1936-37	17.581	4,442	6,957	6.401	2,362
1937-38 . .	18,615	4,442	7,992	6,023	2,719
1938-39	18,236	4,442	6,695	6,711	3,216
1939-40 ...	20,922	4,442	7,863	6,752	3,744
1940-41	24.141	4,442	12,992	3,587	4,846
1941-42	30,768	4,442	16.500	3,528	7,519
1942-43	51,344	4,442	31,911	2,233	13,938
1941-42					
Last Friday of—					
April, 1941	26,712	4,442	10,880	3,606	9,132
May	27,297	4,442	11,380	3,623	9,131
June	27,693	4,442	11,880	3,657	9,131
July	27,301	4,442	12,165	3,765	8,846
August	27,659	4,442	13,163	3,849	7,849
September	28,612	4,442	13,663	3,921	7,650

TABLE NO. 3.—(*Contd.*)

(In lakhs of Rupees)

	Notes in Circulation	Gold Coin & Bullion	Sterling Securities	Rupee Coin	Rupee Securities
1941-42					
Last Friday of—					
October	29,345	4,442	15,567	3,884	6,846
November	30,742	4,442	18,065	3,760	5,647
December	33,560	4,442	22,762	3,418	4,150
January, 1942 ...	35,641	4,442	24,862	3,164	4,150
February	37,968	4,442	27,362	2,948	4,150
March	41,007	4,442	21,285	2,753	13,626
1942-43					
April	44,261	4,442	24,185	2,947	13,822
May	46,065	4,442	25,185	2,779	14,915
June	44,319	4,442	26,185	2,755	12,229
July	45,100	4,442	28,679	2,972	10,237
August	47,425	4,442	31,179	2,873	10,240
September	49,258	4,442	32,979	2,671	10,243
October	51,470	4,442	32,583	2,184	13,239
November	54,036	4,442	35,983	1,530	13,239
December	57,036	4,442	40,483	1,417	12,238
January, 1943 ...	59,325	4,442	35,583	1,458	18,936
February	61,436	4,442	38,573	1,362	18,246
March	64,358	4,442	42,171	1,451	17,447

TABLE NO. 3.—(*Contd.*)

(In lakhs of Rupees)

1943 Average of Friday figures	Notes in Circulation	Gold Coin & Bullion	Sterling Securities	Rupee Coin	Rupee Securities
April, 1943	66,700	4,442	48,079	1,490	13,739
May	69,765	4,442	42,523	1,461	12,445
June	72,025	4,442	55,098	1,572	12,046
July	73,759	4,442	57,398	1,487	11,502
August	75,353	4,442	61,109	1,418	9,462
September	75,975	4,442	63,480	1,456	7,837
October	77,447	4,442	66,559	1,381	6,237
November	79,358	4,442	68,608	1,458	5,833

*All figures are exclusive of Burma.

(Sources: Reserve Bank of India: *Report on Currency and Finance* for the year 1942-43; and the monthly *Statistical Summaries* of the Reserve Bank of India.)

TABLE NO. 4.

Consolidated Position of the Scheduled Banks.

(Source: Monthly Statistical Summary of the Reserve Bank of India).

(In lakhs of Rupees.)

	Demand Liabilities	Time Liabilities	Cash	Balances with Reserve Bank	Advances	Bills Discounted
Annual Average of Friday figures.						
1935-36	12190	9866	595	3186	8770	356
1936-37	12858	10132	601	2627	9511	470
1937-38	13277	10904	661	2462	12343	628
1938-39	12998	10785	664	1594	11585	486
1939-40	13965	10603	708	1743	12589	525
1940-41 .. .	16390	10494	837	3642	12213	384
1941-42	21135	10761	983	3665	12020	493
1942-43	30628	10421	1297	5573	9568	218
Average of Friday figures.						
April 1942	22811	9658	1035	3880	11198	227
May ..	24102	9466	1111	4867	10226	164
June	26101	9656	1252	5873	9725	150
July	27960	9758	1211	6277	8904	169
August	29475	9737	1165	6469	8807	151
September ...	30859	9928	1239	6429	7867	145
October	32164	10224	1263	6540	7925	173

TABLE NO. 4.—(*Contd.*)

(In lakhs of Rupees.)

Average of Friday figures.	Demand Liablities	Time Liabilities	Cash	Balances with Reserve Bank	Advances	Bills Discounted
November ..	33341	10554	1396	6280	8192	226
December ...	33972	10994	1394	5333	9118	279
January, 1943 ..	34471	11369	1517	4873	10023	289
February ...	35998	11799	1482	4852	11055	308
March	37232	12128	1514	5137	12570	353
April	37475	12359	1632	4435	13166	440
May	39087	12595	1751	4950	14135	506
June	41124	12965	1768	5461	14260	494
July	42811	13352	1809	5909	14324	419

TABLE NO. 5

PUBLIC DEBT OF INDIA SINCE 1913-14.

(A)

Rupee Debt (In crores of rupees)

End of March	Un-dated	Over 10 years	Bet-ween 5 and 10 years	Under 5 Years	Trea-sury Bills	P. O. Savings Bank deposits and Cash Certifi-cates	Other obliga-tions	Total
1	2	3	4	5	6	7	8	9
1914	144'52	1'00	...	...	...	23'17	11'08	179'77
1919	143'20	26'42	29'44	59 43	49·24	27·08	24'02	358 78
1924	137'25	29,20	96 93	94'45	51·57	33'21	39 62	482 52
1929	137'41	121'03	50'25	81'54	43 15	56·79	61·04	551'21
1934	126'69	160'73	67'93	79·22	59'24	115 94	83'34	693'09
1939	127'75	129'62	112·70	70'89	46·30	141 46	84'34	709'96
1930	139'93	147'24	113 75	49·35	54·71	185·35	87'48	727'79
1941	148'52	182'98	150 31	95·07	68'00	108'80	106'59	861'17
1942 (Revised)	104'18	261'77	68 75	117 16	136·98	95 55	96 61	941·00
1943 (Prelimi-nary)	245'50	238'41	91'75	172 80	264'70	93'00	102·29	1208'45

(B)

STERLING DEBT*

(In crores of rupees)

End of March	Undated	Over 10 years	Between 5 and 10 years	Under 5 years	Other obliga-tions	Total
1914	265·57	...	...	...	0·24	265'81
1919	257'80	45'96	...	...	0·32	204'08
1924	366 80	28 90	...	...	2·06	397'76
1929	296 61	169'93	4'66	...	1·58	472'78
1934	269'19	198'50	...	43'08	1'38	512'15
1939	268'05	135'11	29·30	32'46	4'18	469'10
1940	255 68	115'44	39'09	28'15	4'18	442 49
1941	24661	40'·1	32 87	20'62	3'82	344·93
1942 (Revised)	134'00	84'66	17'32	20'95	3'77	210'70
1943 (Preliminary)	22'13	4·06	6'88	20'62	3'72	57'41

* Converted at 1 sh 4 d. per rupee upto the end of 1924; and hereafter at 1 sh. 6d.

(**Source:** *Report on Currency and Finance* for the year 1942-43 : Reserve Bank of India.)